BIG BONE LICK

THE MASTODON AT BIG BONE LICK
Painted by Charles R. Knight, The American Museum of Natural History.

BIG BONE LICK

An Outline of Its History
Geology and Paleontology

to which is added an

Annotated Bibliography
of 207 Titles

By
WILLARD ROUSE JILLSON, Sc. D.
Formerly
State Geologist of Kentucky

COMMONWEALTH BOOK COMPANY
St. Martin, Ohio

Copyright © 1936 by Willard Rouse Jillson
Originally published by The Standard Printing Company in 1936
This edition copyright © 2024 by Commonwealth Book Company, Inc.

All rights reserved. No part of this book may be reproduced in any form or by any means without the prior written consent of the publisher, excepting brief quotes used in reviews. Printed in the United States of America.

ISBN: 978-1-948986-76-2

FRONT COVER IMAGE: MASTODON GIGANTEUS, O. JEWITT, CIRCA 1850
COVER MAP: MR. COOPER'S PAPER ON BIG BONE-LICK, 1831
REAR COVER PAINTING: CHARLES R. KNIGHT, 1897

Dedicated

to my friends

John Thomas Lloyd

and

Horace G. Williamson

WILLARD ROUSE JILLSON (May 28, 1890–October 4, 1975) was a Kentucky academic who wrote dozens of books on Kentucky history and geology. Jillson taught at the University of Kentucky in 1918 and later at Transylvania University from 1947 to 1951. He served most notably as Kentucky State Geologist from 1919 to 1932, as the first chairman of the Kentucky State Park Commission from 1924 to 1932, and as director of the Sixth Kentucky Geological Survey.

CONTENTS

		PAGE
I.	Discovery and Exploration	3
II.	Records of the First Travel Journals	15
III.	Early Fossil Collecting and Description	25
IV.	The Jeffersonian Era	47
V.	Later and Recent Collectors	59
VI.	Land Surveys, Grants, and Deeds	77
VII.	Salt Making and Social Activities	87
VIII.	Geology and Paleontology	101
	Bibliography	125
	Index	159

ILLUSTRATIONS

	PAGE
The Mastodon at Big Bone Lick	*Frontispiece*
The Big Bone Country	17
First Survey of Big Bone Lick	76
J. N. Bellin's Map of 1744	*Facing* 90
Big Bone Lick. Cooper's Map of 1831	103

FOREWORD

Kentucky has long been identified with the picturesque, the unusual, the romantic. The earliest white explorers threading their way along its primeval paths during the latter part of the seventeenth century found it to be a glorious land but strangely marked by stern and startling adventure. As the years passed, Frenchmen from the Great Lakes, and Englishmen from beyond the Alleghenies, each in their turn seeking a new course to the west, made leisurely tours down the Ohio. Thus, some two hundred years ago, and in a manner quite natural, came about the discovery of Big Bone Lick—the most extraordinary depository of bones of the great hoofed animals of the Glacial Age in America.

Today, lovers of natural history and pristine conditions look with dismay at the scene surrounding Big Bone Lick where little if anything remains to recall the fame that a century or more ago was part and parcel of this unusual locality. Except for a few crumbling fragments, all of the great bones have vanished and with them the unique atmosphere of the place. Pausing in the deep grass surrounding any of the salt springs one reflects how much too long have the giant fossil treasures of this quaking old bog been the free objective of the curious from all parts of Europe and America. As the years have passed these unreplaceable antiquities have gone to enrich distant museums while the lick area has witnessed a gradual impoverishment. Kentucky has been openly the grand loser in this continual barter of bones but no effective hand or voice has been raised against the practice.

FOREWORD

Big Bone Lick—neglected and despoiled as it has been by one self-seeking generation after another—deserved, and still deserves, a better fate. Marked as one of the cornerstones of early Kentucky history, and widely recognized in those twin sciences, geology and paleontology, this famous salt lick possesses all of the attributes of a monument of natural design. Many bones, suitable for local exhibition, may still be recovered by the employment of careful methods of excavation and preparation. This has been recognized by Dr. Willard Rouse Jillson, whose experience and ability as a geologist and historian have amply qualified him for the writing of this monograph—*Big Bone Lick*. It is hoped that a perusal of these interesting pages may lead to a better understanding and appreciation of Big Bone Lick and the present importance of introducing into this locality some type of permanent conservation and regional improvement.

JOHN URI LLOYD, *President*
Big Bone Lick Association.

Cincinnati, Ohio.
February 10, 1936.

DISCOVERY AND EXPLORATION

I

Discovery and Exploration

"The evident place of death and entombment."

More than two hundred years ago—in 1729 to be exact—an intrepid French Canadian soldier and explorer, then commanding at Fort Niagara, Captain Charles Lemoyne de Longueil,[1] descended the Ohio River from the eastern Great Lakes and discovered Big Bone Lick in Northern Kentucky. His was the military entourage that accompanied and protected the famous French engineer, M. Chaussegros de Lery,[2] whose compass surveys at this time gave basis for the first reconnaissance charting of the meandering course of the Ohio River. Though records do not so state, we may assume without fear of error that he was taken to this remarkable locality by the Indian guides who accompanied him, for this lick in southwestern Boone County was widely known among the aboriginal tribes that inhabited the Ohio Valley.

The Indians, as a matter of fact, relied upon this centrally located spring for much of the salt and a good deal of the game which they required. Up the broad, well-marked buffalo path from the waters of the Ohio they came making regular visitations to this old salty bog to stalk with ease the great hoofed beasts—the buffalo, the deer, and the elk that gathered there to lick the salty earth. And then, after the kill, they lingered in the vicinity to feast upon the carcasses of these animals, cook-

---

[1] Later the Governor of Montreal and Interim Governor of New France; born 1687, died 1759. Commanded Fort Niagara, 1726-1733.

[2] *Remarques sur le Carte de l'Amerique Septentrionale* by Jacques Nicolas Bellin, pp. 120-121, Paris, France, 1755.

ing or dipping them in the sulphur-saline waters which nature here provided in unlimited amount.

In their peculiarly penetrative way these copper-colored savages had, from the earliest time, recognized the therapeutic value of the waters rising in the several original springs at Big Bone. When the first white explorers and pioneers arrived they confirmed the opinions of the native Americans, and from the days of settlement down to the present the waters of Big Bone Lick have been highly regarded for their mildly curative qualities. The first map of Kentucky,[3] prepared by John Filson and published in 1784 in Philadelphia, showed in this area "Salt and Medicinal Springs" and stated, in addition, that "the large bones are found here." Forty years previously —in 1744—Jacques Nicolas Bellin, the celebrated French cartographer, exhibited on his map of Louisiana,[4] published in Paris, this then widely known lick as "the place where they found the elephant bones in 1729."

In the train of M. de Longueil during the next quarter of a century that France continued to exercise domination over the Ohio Valley, many Canadians followed his path and came to Big Bone Lick. The magnificent M. de Celeron, in his lordly movement down the Ohio in 1749, however, missed it, for he turned back to the north at the mouth of the Big Miami.[5] But in this mid-century period, others of western exploratory inclination—notably Englishmen—began to make their way into this storied region. Robert Smith, a resident Indian trader, who lived on the east bank of the Big Miami opposite the Twigtwee town, had been there with others in

[3] *This Map of Kentucke, etc.*, John Filson, Philadelphia, 1784.
[4] *Carte de la Louisiane, etc.*, N. Bellin, Paris, 1744. See p. 90.
[5] *The Ohio Country*, Willard Rouse Jillson, p. 12, Cincinnati, 1932.

1744, as he told Christopher Gist[6] during his journey through central and southern Ohio in 1751.

The unusual spectacle of the "Big Bones" scattered over the ground gave foundation for tales calculated to excite wonder and interest when told by the constantly increasing number of scouts and hunters returning from "the Kentuckie country." Finally, as a few of the bone specimens found their way to the East, the fame of Big Bone Lick became so real that, a full decade before the first guns of the American Revolution sounded along the Atlantic seaboard, this remote and sequestered salt spring in the forested wilderness of the new world had become the subject of spirited conversation, scientific study, and much serious correspondence in Philadelphia, New York, London, Paris, and later throughout Europe.

Colonel Christopher Gist, in the employ of the Ohio Land Company of Virginia, visited Big Bone in 1751. He records in his journal that he secured two large teeth from two men employed by Robert Smith, who, with Hugh Crawford, were just returning from Big Bone. One of these large teeth, evidently from his description taken from the jaw of a mastodon, he "brought in for the Ohio Company." That part of Gist's journal pertinent to Big Bone Lick and vicinity follows:

> (1751) Tuesday 12—I got my Horses over the River and after Breakfast my Boy and I got ferryed over—The Ohio is near ¾ of a Mile wide at Shannoah Town, & is very deep and smooth.
>
> Wednesday 13—We set out S 45 W, down the said River on the SE Side 8M, then S 10 M, here I met two Men

---
[6] *Journal Through Ohio and Kentucky in 1750-51.* C. Gist, Darlington ed. pp. 57-58. Pittsburgh, 1893.

belonging to Robert Smith at whose House I lodged on this Side the Miamee River, and one Hugh Crawford. The said Robert Smith had given Me an order upon these Men, for two of the Teeth of a large Beast which they were bringing from towards the Falls of Ohio, one of which I brought in and delivered to the Ohio Company—Robert Smith informed me that about seven Years ago these Teeth and Bones of three large Beasts (one of which was somewhat smaller than the other two) were found in a Salt Lick or Spring upon a small Creek which runs into the S Side of the Ohio, about 15 M below the Mouth of the great Miamee River, and 20 above the Falls of Ohio. He assured Me that the Rib Bones of the largest of these Beasts were eleven Feet long, and the Skull Bone six feet wide, across the Forehead, & the other bones in Proportion; and that there were several Teeth there, some of which he called Horns, and said they were upwards of five feet long, and as much as a Man could well carry: that he had hid one in a Branch at some Distance from the Place, lest the French Indians should carry it away.

The Tooth which I brought in for the Ohio Company was a Jaw Tooth of better than four Pounds Weight; it appeared to be the furthest Tooth in the Jaw, and looked like fine Ivory when the outside was scraped off—I also met with four Shannoah Indians coming up the River in their Canoes, who informed me that there were about sixty French Indians encamped at the falls.

Monday 18—N 45 W 5 M then SW 20 M, to the lower Salt Lick Creek, which Robert Smith and the Indians told us was about 15 M above the Falls of Ohio; and the Land still hilly the Salt Lick here much the same with those before described this day we heard several Guns which made me imagine the French Indians were not moved, but were still hunting, and firing thereabouts: We also saw some Traps newly set, and the footsteps of some Indians plain on the

Ground as if they had been there the Day before. I was now much troubled that I could not comply with my Instructions, and was once resolved to leave the Boy and Horses, and to go privately on Foot to view the Falls; but the Boy being a poor Hunter, was afraid he would starve if I was long from him, and there was also great Danger lest the French Indians should come upon our Horses Tracts, or hear their Bells, and as I had seen good Land enough, I thought perhaps I might be blamed for venturing so far, in such dangerous Times, so I concluded not to go to the Falls; but Travelled away to the Southward till we were over the little **Cuttaway River.**

During the fall of the following year of 1752, the picturesque John Findley[7] visited Big Bone Lick on a trading expedition. A backwoods figure fully acquainted with the Ohio Indians with whom he had spent several years in the traffic of peltries, he put a stock of goods in canoes, and, accompanied by four white men as helpers, drifted down the Ohio River looking for trade. The adventure was illy timed, just before the beginning of the French and Indian War, and brought upon him disaster, though, at the same time, it fixed his name securely in the history of the new country—*Kentucke*. Finally arriving at the Falls—where Louisville now stands—he became discouraged, having met with no hunting parties of Indians with whom he could barter for their winter catch of furs.

Turning back he went to Big Bone Lick where he met a band of his old friends, the Shawnees, who had just come in from a hunt in Illinois. They asked him to join them at their village, Eskippakithiki[8], in the heart of *Kentucke* where they

---

[7] *John Findley, etc.* Lucien Beckner, Filson Club Quart., Vol. I, p. 113. Louisville, 1927.

[8] *Eskippakithiki, etc.* Lucien Beckner, Filson Club Quart., Vol. 6, p. 372. Louisville, 1932.

promised him good trading in furs. He accepted and journeyed up the Kentucky River to what is now known as the Indian Old Fields in Clark County where he built a house surrounded by a stockade as a headquarters for the oncoming winter's trade in pelts. While living here during the next year or two he became sufficiently impressed and familiar with the terrain of this new and delightful country, the Bluegrass Region of Kentucky, to successfully guide Daniel Boone a few years later— 1769—to the very spot.

Mary Inglis,[9] usually accredited as the first white woman in Kentucky, while an Indian captive, visited Big Bone Lick on a salt-boiling expedition with a party of Shawnees and three Frenchmen, in the autumn of 1756. Having been previously separated from her two little boys at the Indian village at the mouth of the Scioto, she determined to escape. It is related that, as she was about to leave the lick, she traded her tomahawk with one of the Frenchmen in the company, who at the time was "sitting on one of the big bones cracking walnuts." Taking the buffalo path to the Ohio, she made her way directly up stream and, after many hardships, finally arrived at the outlying settlements of Montgomery County, Virginia. Thirteen years afterwards one of her sons was recovered, but the other, unable to withstand the severities of Indian life, died in captivity.

Nearly a decade later Colonel George Croghan,[10] who undoubtedly had known about this lick many years, came to Big Bone in the course of his active western explorations.

[9] *History of Kentucky.* Richard Collins, Vol. II, pp. 53 and 54. Covington, 1882.
[10] *Journey Down the Ohio in 1765.* G. Croghan in *History of Kentucky.* Butler, 1834.

BIG BONE LICK

While here he made the first considerable collection of bones of record. Captain Harry Gordon[11] followed in 1766, and, at the instance of Croghan, made a representative collection, portions of which, consisting chiefly of the mastodon and the mammoth, were sent to Lord Shelbourne and Dr. Benjamin Franklin in London, England.[12] But these were only a few— though, perhaps, among the most notable of those who made it their business to investigate this unusual locality during those troublous times immediately preceding and shortly following the old French and Indian War. To the French *cour de bois* and the English Indian traders, it was a point as well known as the Falls of the Ohio or the portage at the Pickawillany on the headwaters of the Miami and the Auglaize.

During all of these years of colonial struggle, and stretching backward endlessly into the long period antedating the coming of the first white man into the Ohio Valley, the Indians living south of the Great Lakes were frequent visitors to Big Bone. The great animal paths that led through the forest to it, the immense herds of deer and buffalo that gathered there for the salt, and the spectacle of the big bones whitening in the sun, were particulars with which they were intimately familiar. As evidence of this we have but to turn to the simple yet accurate description of the lick and its environs which was given by some Shawnees[13] to Colonel Boquette at Fort du Quesne prior to 1762. Or, if further proof were needed, it may be seen in

---

[11] *Journey Down the Ohio in 1766.* H. Gordon, Shelbourne MSS. Pub. Archives of Canada, Vol. 48, pp. 159-178. 1767.

[12] *Of Some Very Large Fossil Teeth Found in North America.* Peter Collinson, Phil. Trans. Royal Soc. London. Vol. LVII, pp. 464 and 468. London, 1767; Reprint abridged, Vol. XII, pp. 476, 477, 478. London, 1809.

[13] *Archaeological Americanae Tellevies Collectanea et Specimina*, etc., by Benjamin Smith Barton. Pp. 34-40. Philadelphia, 1814.

the legend told by the Delaware warriors to the Governor of Virginia during the American Revolution. Thomas Jefferson has recorded that, when asked as to the great animal whose bones were found at the salt licks on the Ohio, the chief spokesman of his savage visitors drew himself up to oratorical station and said:[14]

"In ancient times a herd of these tremendous animals came to the Big-bone licks, and began an universal destruction of the bear, deer, elks, buffaloes, and other animals which had been created for the use of the Indians: that the Great Man above, looking down and seeing this, was so enraged that he seized his lightning, descended on the earth, seated himself on a neighboring mountain, on a rock of which his seat and the print of his feet are still to be seen, and hurled his bolts among them till the whole were slaughtered, except the big bull, who presenting his forehead to the shafts, shook them off as they fell; but missing one at length, it wounded him in the side; whereon, springing round, he bounded over the Ohio, over the Wabash, the Illinois, and finally over the great lakes, where he is living at this day."

Distinguished by aboriginal legend and colonial exploitation, sought out by learned and ignorant alike, what, it may be fairly asked, gave such early notoriety to this bit of swamp land? What circumstances brought it to the forefront of scientific investigation the world around during the last century and a half, and causes it to maintain its outstanding preeminence even to this day? The answer is not hard to find. It is written in its brief but telling name—Big Bone. These relics, fossils of a vast assemblage of great beasts gathered here

---
[14] *Notes on the State of Virginia.* Thomas Jefferson. Pp. 18-80. R. T. Rawle, Philadelphia, 1801.

during the glacial age, focused world attention upon this lick. When the first white man came—call him de Longueil or name some predecessor, possibly La Salle, whose tour through this part of the virgin west has long since been forgotten—Big Bone Lick was the very evident place of death and entombment of many of the largest mammals that ever coursed the American wilderness.

RECORDS OF THE FIRST
TRAVEL JOURNALS

II
Records of the First Travel Journals

"A D—d Irish rascal has broken a piece of my elephant tooth."

One of the most interesting early descriptions of **Big Bone Lick** is that found in the travel journal of Colonel George Croghan. This description intrigues the imagination because it was written in 1765 at the time he was making the first extensive collection of big bones from this locality. Croghan was employed by the colony of Pennsylvania as an Indian Agent and, as all records go to prove, was one of the most able Englishmen in this capacity that ever braved the perils of the savage-infested wilderness. After reciting the details of his journey with a party down the Ohio from Fort Pitt (Pittsburgh) which he left May 15, 1765, he wrote the following notes on **Big Bone Lick**:

> We passed the Great Miame River, about thirty miles from the little river of that name, and in the evening arrived at the place where the Elephants' bones are found, where we encamped, intending to take a view of the place next morning. This day we came about seventy miles. The country on both sides level, and rich bottoms well watered.
>
> Early in the morning we went to the great Lick, where those bones are only found, about four miles from the river, on the south-east side. In our way we passed through a fine timbered clear wood; we came into a large road which the Buffaloes have beaten, spacious enough for two wagons to go abreast, and leading straight into the Lick. It appears that there are vast quantities of these bones lying five or six feet under the ground, which we discovered in the bank, at the

edge of the Lick. We found here two tusks above six feet long; we carried one, with some other bones, to our boats, and set off.

But travel in the western wilderness during these early times was fraught with great peril for even so astute a man as Colonel Croghan. Scarcely a week after his visit to Big Bone Lick, he and his party were set upon by a band of eighty Kickapoos and Mascoutins on the Ohio below the Wabash near the lower Shawnee town. These unfriendly Algonquin Indians quickly captured them and plundered them. Narrowly escaping death, Croghan and his men found their way back to Fort Pitt, but his collection of fossils, the first of any size to be taken from Big Bone Lick, was lost.[1] Nevertheless, a year later, he had patched up a peace treaty with the Ohio Indians at meetings held at Fort Pitt and Detroit. Directly following these agreements he again set out down the Ohio for the Illinois country accompanied by a military entourage which included two very intelligent young men, one an army engineer, Captain Harry Gordon, and the other his associate, a geographer, Ensign Thomas Hutchins. These men were assigned to this expedition into the wilderness by General Gage to prepare maps and report on the military situation in the west. From the interesting journal of Captain Gordon, written on this trip in 1766—three years before Daniel Boone, led by the resolute Finley,* first passed through the Cumberland Gap to view the fertile land of Kentucky—we take this unique primeval picture[2] of Big Bone:

[1] *The Story of the Discovery of Big Bone Lick.* E. Kindle, Ky. Geol. Survey, Series VI, Vol. 31, pp. 189-212. Frankfort, 1931.
 *Spelled both *Findley* and *Finley,* usually the latter.
[2] *Journey Down the Ohio in 1766.* H. Gordon, Shelbourne MSS., Vol. 48, pp. 159-178. Pub. Archives, Canada, 1767.

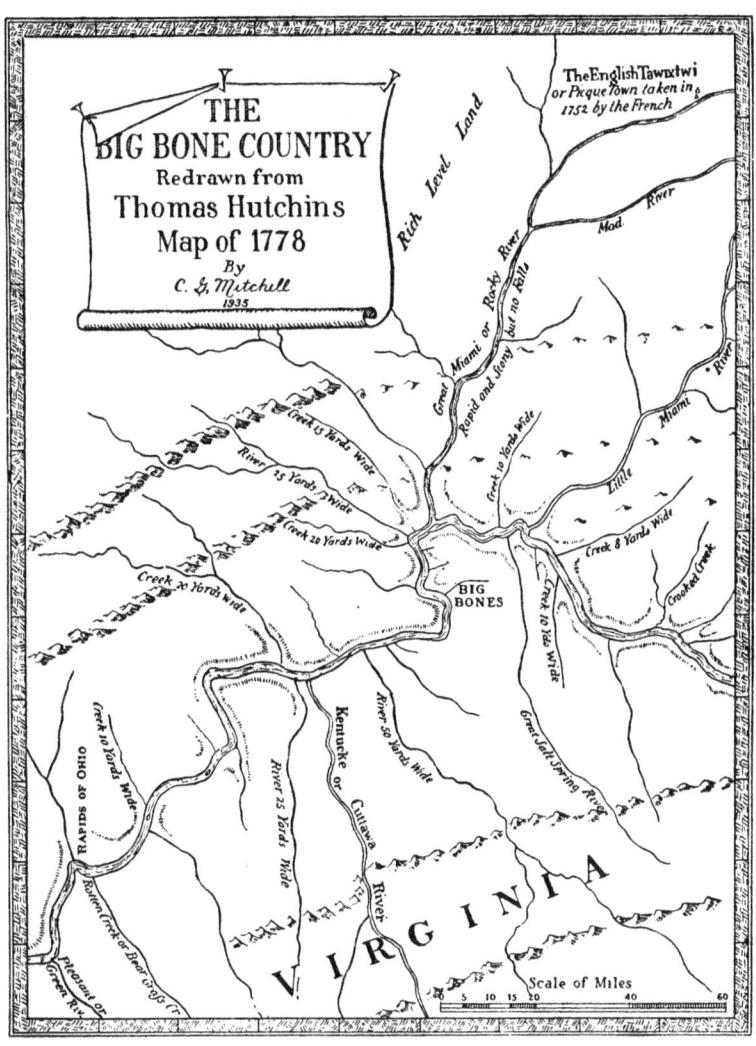

The mountain ranges indicated in Southeastern Indiana and Northern Kentucky are illustrative of the defectiveness of cartographic knowledge as to the transmontane west current among American geographers during the early and middle part of the eighteenth century.

We encamped opposite the great lick, and next day I went with a Party of Indians and Batteau-Men to view this much-talked-of Place. The beaten Roads from all Quarters to it easily conducted Us: they resemble those to an Inland Village where cattle go to and fro a large Common. The Pasturage near it seems of the finest kind, mixed with Grass and Herbage, and well watered; on our Arrival at the Lick which is 5 miles distance South of the River, we discovered laying about many large Bones, some of which the exact Patterns of Elephants Tusks, & others of different parts of a large Animal. The extent of the Muddy part of the Lick is ¾ of an acre; this Mud being of a salt quality is greedily lick'd by Buffalo, Elk & Deer, who came from distant parts, in great Numbers for this purpose; we picked up several of the Bones, some out of ye Mud, others off the Ground; returned, proceeded next Day & arrived at the Falls 19th July.

An even dozen years later—in 1778—Hutchins' explorations and observations in the west were brought together in the form of a map which was published in London under the title, *A New Map of the Western Parts of Virginia, Pennsylvania, Maryland, and North Carolina.* On this new chart of the west, which, more than anything else he did in a lifetime of active civil and military service, has caused his name to be remembered, he took care to locate the celebrated Kentucky salt spring and fossil locality which he visited with Captain Gordon in 1766, by the simple but effective designation of "Big Bone." Together with his map he published a brief piece of writing descriptive of the topography of the west. Within the covers of this old and yellowing pamphlet[3] appears the

---

[3] *A Topographical Description of the Western Parts of Virginia, Pennsylvania, Maryland, and North Carolina.* Thomas Hutchins, pp. 82 and 83. London, 1778. Reprinted by F. C. Hicks. Cleveland, 1904.

following early picture of Big Bone Lick and its geographical surroundings:

> About 584 miles below Fort Pitt, and on the eaftern fide of the Ohio River, about three miles from it, at the head of a fmall Creek or Run, where are feveral large and miry Salt Springs, are found numbers of large bones, teeth and tusks, commonly fuppofed to be thofe of Elephants:—but the celebrated Doctor Hunter of London, in his ingenious and curious Obferations of thefe bones, & ect. has fuppofed them to belong to fome Carnivorous animal, larger than an ordinary Elephants.*
>
> *See Philosophical Transactions, 1768.

In the mid-summer of 1773 when Captain Thomas Bullitt[4] and Hancock Taylor, with the brothers, James, George, and Robert McAfee, James McCoun and Samuel Adams, arrived at Big Bone on their first exploratory and surveying excursion down the Ohio and into *Kentucke,* the ribs and vertebrae of the vanished glacial elephants were so numerous and of such enormous size that the party occupied themselves by making seats and tent poles of these gigantic fossils. Robert McAfee[5] has left a very interesting personal comment on Big Bone Lick. He said in his journal of 1773:

> The 3d [of July] we lay there [on the Ohio] and the 4th we came up the river about 10 miles to make a station and survey land. On the 5th, we went to see the Big Bone, which is a wonder to see the large bones that lie there, which have been of several large big creatures. The lick is about 200 yards long and as wide, and the waters and mud are of

---
[4] *History of Kentucky,* Richard Collins, Vol. I, p. 17. Covington, 1882.
[5] *Journal of an Exploration Through Kentucky in 1773,* Robert McAfee in Woods-McAfee Memorial, pp. 433 and 445. Louisville, 1905.

a sulphur smell. There are several other licks on the same creek, and the same taste and smell; and there is very fine land on the same creek which was surveyed that day.

In the fall of the same year, James Douglas, another pioneer surveyor of Kentucky, visited this celebrated fossil locality and found the ten acres constituting the lick bare of trees and herbage of every kind. He reported, like all the others, that large numbers of bones of the mastodon and the mammoth lay scattered upon the ground.

Much the same scene greeted the eye of Thomas Hanson about a year later when he arrived at Big Bone with the surveyors John Floyd and James Douglas in the late spring of 1774. He wrote as follows in his journal:[6]

> [May] 12th. We proceeded down to a Creek 8 miles which lies within 3 miles of the Big Bone Lick. There was 1000 acres surveyed for William Christian, about the Lick. The land is not so good as the other Bottoms, likewise a little broken. There is a number of large Teeth to [be] seen about this Lick, which the People imagined to be Elephants. There is one Seven Feet and three Inches long. It is nine inches in Diameter at one End and five inches at the other.
>
> 13th. Mr. Douglass made a survey of 2000 acres on the upper side of the Creek for Mr. William Christian, good land. At Mr. Douglasses return, we embarked and floated down the River to Kentucky, 47 miles and by daybreak landed. In our passage we came to an Indian Camp landed and found two Delewares, and a Squaw, we gave them some Corn and Salt.

Among the several early descriptions of Big Bone Lick the one given by Nicholas Cresswell, in his journal of 1775, is of

---

[6] *Journal Kept on the River Ohio in the Year 1774.* T. Hanson, p. 121 in Thwaites and Kellogg's *Dunmore's War*. Madison, 1905.

great value because of its clarity and wealth of detail. Returning upstream from the vicinity of Harrod's Fort—now Harrodsburg—he visited with others the widely known salt lick and wrote:[7]

> SATURDAY, JUNE 17th. This morning set out for the Elephant Bone Lick, which is only three miles S. E. of the River. However, we lost our way and I suppose travelled twenty miles before we found it. Where the bones are found is a large muddy pond, a little more than knee deep with a Salt spring in it which I suppose preserves the bones sound. Found several bones of a Prodigious size, I take them to be Elephants, for we found a part of a tusk, about two feet long, Ivory to all appearance, but by length of time had grown yellow and soft. All of us stripped and went into the pond to grabble for teeth and found several. Joseph Passiers found a Jaw tooth which he gave me. It was judged by the company to weigh 10 pounds. I got a shell of a Tusk of hard and good ivory about eighteen inches long. There is a great number of bones in a Bank on the side of this pond of an enormous size but decayed and rotten. Ribs 9 inches broad, Thigh bones 10 inches diameter. What sort of animals these were is not clearly known. All the traditionary accounts by the Indians is that they were White Buffaloes that killed themselves by drinking salt water. It appears to me from the shape of their teeth that they were Grass-eaters. There neither is or ever were any Elephants in North or South America, that I can learn, or any quadruped one tenth part as large as these was, if one may be allowed to judge from the appearance of these bones, which must have been considerably larger than they are now. Captn. Hancock Lee told me he had found a tusk here that was six feet long, very sound but yellow. These tusks are like those brought from the Coast of Africa. Saw some Buffaloes but

---

[7] *Journal of Nicholas Cresswell, 1774-1777.* Pp. 76, 88, 89. New York, 1928.

killed none. Several Indian paintings on the trees. Got plenty of Mulberries, very sweet and pleasant fruit but bad for the teeth. One of the company shot a Deer. The loudest Thunder and heaviest rain I ever saw this afternoon. Got to the Camp well wet and most heartily tired. A D—d Irish rascal has broken a piece of my Elephant tooth, put me in a violent passion, can write no more.

EARLY FOSSIL COLLECTING AND DESCRIPTION

III

Early Fossil Collecting and Description

"The tyrant of the forests, the devourer of man."—Filson.

The first mammalian fossils removed from Big Bone Lick, of which there is any positive record, were those taken away by the Indian trader, Robert Smith, whose residence, during the middle of the eighteenth century, was on the east side of the Big Miami River at Pickawillany. It will be recalled that, in 1751, he told Christopher Gist[1] he had been to Big Bone Lick seven years previously—in 1744—and had removed several bones including one giant tusk "upwards of five feet long," which he found there. What became of this first collection is unknown. It is entirely probable that it was lost within a short time, for the French sacked and burned the village and stockade at Pickawillany in 1752* and then, for good measure, killed, dismembered, and cooked the body of "Old Britain," the then much respected chief of the Miamis.

Colonel Gist's collection from Big Bone in 1751 was so small as to be negligible; and this may be said for each of the several others visiting the lick until Colonel George Croghan came in 1765. At this time, according to Croghan, a considerable number of select fossils were removed from the lick. It is extremely unfortunate that this early collection was lost, shortly thereafter, in Croghan's serious engagement with the French Indians near the mouth of the Wabash. The loss of these bones on the lower Ohio, however, made Croghan more

---
[1] *Journal Through Ohio and Kentucky in 1750-51.* C. Gist, Darlington ed. pp. 57-58. Pittsburgh, 1893.
**The Ohio Country.* Willard Rouse Jillson, p. 13. Cincinnati, 1932.

determined than ever to get some fossils from this locality, during his second western expedition which was undertaken during the following year, 1766. At the appropriate time orders were issued to his lieutenant and, during their visit to Big Bone Lick, a collection of the giant fossils was made by Captain Gordon and his Indian guides. These bones were sent by Colonel Croghan to New York, and thence to London where a portion of them were delivered to Lord Shelbourne, minister to the American Colonies, and the remainder to Doctor Franklin. Evidently greatly intrigued by this unusual present of bones from America's undeveloped west, the energetic Franklin immediately examined them and then penned the following letter[2] to their donor in America:

London, 5 August, 1767

Col. George Croghan:
Sir:

I return you many thanks for the box of elephants' tusks and grinders. They are extremely curious on many accounts; no living elephant having been seen in any part of America by any of the Europeans settled there, or remembered in any tradition of the Indians. It is also puzzling to conceive what should have brought so many of them to die on the same spot; and that no such remains should be found in any other part of the continent, except in that very distant country, Peru, from whence some grinders of the same kind, formerly brought, are now in the museum of the Royal Society. The tusks agree with those of the African and Asiatic elephant in being nearly of the same form and texture, and some of them, notwithstanding the length of time they must have lain, being still good ivory. But the grinders differ, being full of Knobs, like the grinders of a carnivorous

---

[2] *The Works of Benjamin Franklin.* Edited by John Bigelow, Federal Edition, Vol. IV, pp. 303-304. New York and London, 1904.

animal; when those of the elephant, who eats only vegetables, are almost smooth. But then we know of no other animal with tusks like an elephant, to whom such grinders might belong.

It is remarkable, that elephants now inhabit naturally only hot countries where there is no winter, and yet these remains are found in a winter country; and it is no uncommon thing to find elephants' tusks in Siberia, in great quantities, when their rivers overflow, and wash away the earth, though Siberia is still more a wintry country than that on the Ohio; which looks as if the earth had anciently been in another position, and the climates differently placed from what they are at present.

With great regard, I am, Sir,
Your most obedient humble servant,
B. FRANKLIN.

Not satisfied with his own conclusions, which as we now know were quite correct, Franklin continued his investigation touching upon the big bones from *Kentucke*. A year later, in 1768, we find him addressing the following letter[3] to the celebrated Abbe Chappe on this subject:

London, Jan. 31, 1768.
ABBE CHAPPE.[4]
Sir:

I sent you sometime since, directed to the Care of M. Molini, a Bookseller near the Quay des Augustins, a Tooth

---

[3] *The Writings of Benjamin Franklin.* Ed. by Albert H. Smith. Vol. 5, p. 92.

[4] Abbe Chappe D'Auteroche (1722-1769), astronomer and author of *"Voyage en Siberie" (1768).* He was sent to Tobolsk to observe the transit of Venus (1761).

that I mentioned to you when I had the pleasure of meeting with you at the Marquis de Courtanvaux's. It was found near the River Ohio in America, about 200 Leagues below Fort du Quesne, at what is called the Great Licking Place, where the Earth has a Saltish Taste that is agreeable to the Buffaloes and Deer, who come there at certain Seasons in great Numbers to lick the same. At this Place have been found the Skeletons of near 30 large Animals suppos'd to be Elephants, several Tusks like those of Elephants being found with these Grinder Teeth—Four of these Grinders were sent me by the Gentleman[5] who brought them from the Ohio to New York, together with 4 Tusks, one of which is 6 Feet long and in the thickest Part near 6 inches Diameter, and also one of the Vertebrae—My Lord Shelbourn receiv'd at the same time 3 or four of them with a Jaw Bone & one or two Grinders remaining in it. Some of Our Naturalists here, however, contend that these are not the Grinders of Elephants but of some carnivorous Animal unknown, because such Knobs or Prominences on the Face of the Tooth are not to be found on those of Elephants, and only, as they say, on those of carnivorous Animals. But it appears to me that Animals capable of carrying such large & heavy Tusks, must themselves be large Creatures, too bulky to have the Activity necessary for pursuing and taking Prey; and therefore I am inclin'd to think those Knobs are only a small Variety. Animals of the same kind and Name often differing more materially, and that those Knobs might be as useful to grind the small branches of Trees, as to chaw Flesh—However I should be glad to have your Opinion, and to know from you whether any of the kind have been found in Siberia.

      With great Esteem & Respect, I am
    Sir
        Your most obedt huml
         Servant
          B. F.

---

[5] Colonel George Croghan.

Peter Collinson of London after viewing these American fossils reported upon them at some length to the Royal Society[6] in 1767. Particular as to their enumeration, he has described them in the following quaint fashion:

To Lord Shelburne—Two of the largest tusks or teeth, one whole and entire, about 6 feet long, the thickness of common elephant's teeth; a jaw-bone, with 2 of them in it.

To Dr. Franklin—Four great tusks, of different sizes. One broken in halves, near 6 feet long. One much decayed, the center looks like chalk or lime. A part was cut off from one of these teeth, that has all the appearance of fine white ivory. A joint of the vertebrae. Three of the large pronged teeth; one has 4 rows of fangs.

Protruding from the barren, muchly trodden earth about the lick and embedded in the salty ooze surrounding it at various depths down to the gravelled bed of Big Bone Creek, which made its way through the area, were the great tusks, the limb and the rib bones of two major varieties of extinct elephants—the mammoth and the mastodon. Interspersed among these great fossils (many of which, particularly the proboscidian skulls, were of such size as to be beyond the handling of any man) the early explorers found numerous detached skeletal remains of other gigantic animals. Here were bones of the glacial horse, the ground sloth, the arctic ox, and the early and the contemporary buffalo, the caribou, the moose, the elk, the reindeer, and the bear. Some prostrate and whitening in the sun and weather, others partly buried in the mud or water-soaked in the bed of the creek of the salty pools surrounding

---

[6] *Of Some Very Large Fossil Teeth Found in North America.* Peter Collinson. Phil. Trans. Royal Soc. of London. Vol. LVII, p. 464. London, 1767; Reprint Vol. XII, pp. 476-478. London, 1809.

these springs themselves, it was all in all the greatest natural depository of the bones of the great Pleistocene mammals that man's eye had ever beheld in any part of the world.

Small wonder that early travellers on these western waters went out of their way to behold it, or, in passing, picked up a great tooth or an ivory tusk to be laboriously freighted by trail or by stream back to civilization. Less wonder that the many-sided Benjamin Franklin[7] in London in 1767, should be examining and writing about some of these relics of a lost proboscidian race, or that George Louis de Clerc de Buffon,[8] the great French naturalist, should, shortly thereafter, be describing some of these quaint American bones and teeth, in Paris, France.

The first general description of Big Bone Lick to appear in an American book was penned by John Filson, the engaging school teacher-explorer of Chester County, Pennsylvania. In his precious prose poem, *The Discovery, Settlement, and Present State of Kentucke*[9] (Wilmington, 1784), the following unusually speculative lines appeared:

> At a salt spring near Ohio River, very large bones are found, far surpassing the size of any species of animal now in America. The head appears to have been about three feet long, the ribs seven, and the thigh bones about four; one of which is reposited in the library at Philadelphia, and said to weigh 78 pounds. The tusks are above a foot in length, the grinders about five inches square and eight inches long.

---

[7] *Works of Benjamin Franklin.* J. Sparks, pp. 275-276, Vol. VI. Boston, 1840. Also *Writings of Benjamin Franklin.* A. H. Smith, p. 92, Vol. V.

[8] *Geology of Kentucky.* A. M. Miller, p. 220. Frankfort, 1919.

[9] *The Discovery, Settlement, and Present State of Kentucke.* John Filson, pp. 33-36. Wilmington, 1784.

These bones have equally excited the amazement of the ignorant, and attracted the attention of the philosopher. Specimens of them have been sent both to France and England, where they have been examined with the greatest diligence, and found upon comparison to be the remains of the same species of animals that produced those other fossil bones which have been discovered in Tartary, Chili, and several other places, both of the old and new continent. What animal this is, and by what means its ruins are found in regions so widely different, and where none exists at present, is a question of more difficult decision. The ignorant and superstitious Tartars attribute them to a creature which they call Maimon, who, they say, usually resides at the bottom of the rivers, and of whom they relate many marvelous stories; but as this is an assertion totally divested of proof, and even of probability, it has justly been rejected by the learned; and on the other hand it is certain that no such amphibious animal exists in our American waters. The bones themselves bear a great resemblance to those of the elephant. There is no other terrestrial animal now known large enough to produce them. The tusks with which they are equally furnished, equally produce true ivory. These external resemblances have generally made superficial observers conclude that they could belong to no other than that prince of quadrupeds; and when they first drew attention of the world, philosophers seem to have subscribed to the same opinion. But if so, whence is it that the whole species has disappeared from America? An animal so laborious and so docile, that the industry of the Peruvians, which reduced to servitude and subjected to education species so vastly inferior in those qualities, as the llama and the paca, could ever have overlooked the elephant, if he had been to be found in their country. Whence is it that these bones are found in climates where the elephant, a native of the torrid zone, cannot even subsist in his wild state, and in a state of servitude will not propagate? These are difficulties sufficient to stagger credulity itself; and at length produced the enquiries of Dr. Hunter. That celebrated anatomist, having procured specimens from the Ohio, examined them with that accuracy for which he is so much distinguished. He discovered a considerable difference between the shape and structure of the bones and those of the elephant. He observed from the form of the teeth that they must have belonged to a carnivorous animal; whereas the habits of the elephant are foreign to such sustenance, and his jaws totally unprovided with the teeth necessary for its use, and from the whole he concluded, to the satisfaction of naturalists, that these bones belonged to a quadruped now unknown, and whose race is probably extinct, unless it may be found in the extensive continent of New Holland, whose recesses have not yet been pervaded by the curiosity or avidity of civilized man. Can then so great a link have perished from the chain of nature? Happy we that it has. How formidable an enemy to the human species, an animal as large as the elephant, the tyrant of the forests, perhaps the devourer of man. Nations, such as the Indians, must have been in perpetual alarm. The animosities among the various tribes must have been suspended till the common enemy who threatened the very existence of all should be extirpated. To this circumstance we are probably indebted for a fact, which is perhaps singular in its kind, the extinction of a whole race of animals from the system of nature.

Nearly a decade later, in 1793, another book describing a portion of the interior of North America appeared. It was issued from the press of J. Debrett in London, England, and Captain Gilbert Imlay[10] was the author. In it occur the following lines touching upon Big Bone Lick:

> Between the mouths of the Licking and Kentucky lies the Great Bone Lick, which is justly celebrated for the

[10] *Topographical Description of the Western Territory of North America.* G. Imlay, pp. 47 and 48, and p. 236. London, 1793.

remarkable bones which are found there, and which gave name to the place. Several of these bones have been sent to Europe; but I believe no person who has written upon natural history has given any decided opinion as to what class of animal they belonged. Buffon has called them the "Mammouth"; but I am at a loss to know from what authority, as we have no tradition either oral or written, that gives an account of any species of animals which were as large as those must have been, judging by the magnitude of the bones. Buffon says that similar bones have been found both in Ireland (if I am not mistaken) and in some part of Asia. It appears somewhat extraordinary, at the first view, that we should discover manifest proofs of there having existed animals of which we can form no adequate idea, and which in size must have far exceeded anything now known upon earth; and those signs, too, in climates where the elephant (the largest animal now in existence) is never found. Every phenomenon upon the earth tends to confirm the idea, that it ever has been subject to revolutions, besides its diurnal and annual motion from east to west.

I have already taken notice of the great bones which have been found in this country; but as I was not minute as to the estimate of their size I shall just remark that it was the opinion of your celebrated anatomist, the late Dr. Hunter, from an examination of the tusks, that the mammouth was an animal entirely different from the elephant; and Mr. Jefferson, who seems to have examined the skeleton with curious attention, says, "The bones bespeak an animal of five or six times the cubic volume of the elephant, as Mons. de Buffon has admitted." And I have been informed by a gentleman who attended the lectures of Dr. Cline, in London, that this ingenious anatomist used to produce one of the tusks of the mammouth when lecturing and declared that the animal must have been carnivorous.

In 1795 General William Henry Harrison[11] made a collection of bones from this famous lick that filled thirteen hogsheads, but, unfortunately, while being freighted by river to the East, this precious cargo capsized below Pittsburgh and was lost. The French General Colland[12] also made a collection at Big Bone about this same time. A small but fine collection of these bones came into the hands of Thomas Jefferson about 1797, and he became an ardent paleontologist as his long-to-be remembered paper on the great glacial ground sloth, *Megatherium jeffersoni,* presented before the American Philosophical Society in Philadelphia, amply attests. By his orders some of these remarkable Kentucky bones were later sent as a token of American esteem to Georges Cuvier, the outstanding French anatomist and paleontologist, who published on them in Paris.

In 1804 Dr. William Goforth,[13] of Cincinnati, carefully worked the locality of these salt springs and made a large and comprehensive collection of proboscidian fossils. Thomas Ashe, the celebrated English traveller and writer, passing through the Ohio Valley, came into possession of these bones by agreement with Goforth in 1806, and took them via New Orleans to England. After exhibiting them in the Liverpool Museum and elsewhere, he sold these relics, pocketed the money, and forgot his obligation to Goforth, in far-away America. Part of this group of giant fossils collected by the industrious Dr. Goforth are now in London in the Royal College of Surgeons. The remainder was divided between Professor Mon-

---

[11] *Notices of Big-Bone Lick.* William Cooper, Month. Am. Jour. Geol., Vol. I, pp. 158-174. October, 1831. *Story of the Discovery of Big Bone Lick.* E. Kindle, Ky. Geol. Survey, Ser. VI, Vol. 31, pp. 189-212. Frankfort, 1931. Also O. P. Hay, p. 401. 1923.

[12] *Ibid.*

[13] *History of Kentucky.* L. Collins, pp. 180-181. Maysville, 1850.

roe of Edinburgh and Dr. Blake of Dublin and, at the present time, if still intact, cannot be located. The following comment taken from an early issue of the *Navigator*, which was published in Pittsburgh, gives a good contemporary view of the low esteem in which Mr. Ashe was held in this country as a result of his theft of these fossils from Big Bone Lick. A thoroughgoing rascal he must have been indeed, for it appears from this piece of writing that he did not confine his thievery to big bones but openly practiced one of the lowest arts—literary piracy. The *Navigator's* writer said:[14]

> I forgive Mr. Ash* for this "literary theft" as the practice has become common nowadays, but I am not going to forgive him for the bone theft he committed on my friend Doctor Goforth,—then of Cincinnati, now of the city of New Orleans—than whom a better man does not exist, and the last man in America, Mr. Ash ought to have thus basely deceived and cheated, for in his house he ate of his bread, and partook of his friendship and hospitality while a stranger and sojourner in the land. The particulars of this circumstance are briefly this: Dr. Goforth had for several years been engaged in collecting the mammoths and other enormous bones at the Big Bone Lick in Kentucky and at an expense of much time, labor, and many hundreds of dollars. In the year 1804 or 1805 he conveyed about 5 tons of these bones to Pittsburgh with a view of transporting them to Philadelphia and sell them to Mr. Peale, or to the American Philosophical Society. The bones, however, remained in Pittsburgh some time.
>
> Mr. Ash had passed through Pittsburgh and descended to Cincinnati. There learning that Doctor Goforth had a very valuable collection of Big Bones he soon ingratiated himself into the Dr.'s graces, and entered into written arti-

---

[14] *The Navigator.* By Zadok Cramer, pp. 201-204. Pittsburgh, 1814.
*Spelled *Ash* and *Ashe,* usually the latter.

cles with him to become his agent for the sale of the bones, he being allowed a specified part of the clear profits of sale, and New Orleans being fixed upon as the market for their disposal. Accordingly, Mr. Ash returned to Pittsburgh in 1806-07 with an order from Dr. Goforth for the bones. They had been deposited with the late Dr. Richardson, who delivered them to Mr. Ash or Arvil, the name he then went by. The bones were boated to Cincinnati, under the command of Mr. Ash, thence he proceeded to New Orleans, where he made a feint to sell them, and was offered seven thousand dollars for them.

He observed that that sum was not 1/10 of the value and from New Orleans shipped them to London, where, no doubt, he has accumulated an immense fortune by exhibiting that great natural treasure of curiosities to the court of that metropolis, while their real owner here is laboring under all difficulties of the loss of so valuable a property. Thus Mr. Ash, a poor adventurer from Ireland, who introduced himself at Pittsburgh in 1806, wishing to take up a school for the education of children, is now seen at the court of London, exhibiting Dr. Goforth's Mammoth Bones and writing books defaming America and its citizens.

President Thomas Jefferson's fundamental interest as a paleontologist in the fossils of Big Bone Lick, beginning during the last years of the eighteenth century, gradually ripened into a strong desire to possess and examine a more representative collection from this celebrated Kentucky locality than had heretofore been available to him. Accordingly, in 1806, when he found himself in the White House as the young nation's Chief Executive, he had his personal friend, Dr. Caspar Wistar, Secretary of the American Philosophical Society of Philadelphia, write Dr. Goforth, in Cincinnati, the following letter[15]

---

[15] *The Navigator.* By Zadok Cramer, pp. 201-204. Pittsburgh, 1814.

BIG BONE LICK

of inquiry as to the fossils which he had collected and others still available at Big Bone Lick:

Philadelphia, Dec. 1, 1806

Dr. William Goforth

Sir:

I beg leave to address you on the part of the American Philosophical Society, to request that you would favor the members of that institution with a description of the Bones of a large animal with claws, which you have procured in the western country—The accounts which have been circulated by travelers respecting the size of the foot have particularly attracted our attention. We have been induced (by information from the same source) to believe that some bones of the mammoth were in your collection—Being possessed of all the bones of that animal, except those of the head, we will only ask you for information of that part of the mammoth—but an account of all the other unknown bones will be interesting to us.

At the same time, I beg leave to ask your opinion respecting the probability of procuring more of those bones, and your advice concerning the method of attempting it.

If your avocations will permit you to favor the society with an answer, please address it to the President of the U. S. who is President of the Society.

With great respect,
I am your friend and servant—
Caspar Wistar, Jun.

A continuation of this correspondence indicates that Dr. Goforth was at heart more of a collector and paleontologist than he was a physician. Acting upon the suggestions of Dr. Wistar, he shortly replied[16] as follows to the President at Washington:

[16] *The Navigator.* By Zadok Cramer, pp. 201-204. Pittsburgh, 1814.

Cincinnati, Ohio
[1807?]

Thomas Jefferson, Esq.
President of the United States.
Respected Sir,

I received a letter from Caspar Wistar Jun. dated 1st of Dec. 1806, on behalf of the American Philosophical Society of Philadelphia requesting information concerning the head of the mammoth; the bones of a large animal with claws; an account of other unknown bones; and also my opinion of the probability of procuring more bones, and the method of attempting it—and I was desired to address my answer to you.

The bones I collected were unfortunately intrusted to the care of a person who descended the Mississippi with them some months since; whether he proceeded to Europe with them, I am ignorant, as from accident or some other cause, I have received no account either of him or them.— My answer cannot therefore be expected to contain accurate or exact descriptions of the bones, but such a general description as I can give from memory, follows: The part of a head which was in my possession, and which I thought to be the head of the mammoth, appeared small. I only possessed the maxilla superior, and maxilla inferior with the teeth,—two on each side of the jaw,—the 2 nearest the jaw were molars, and had two points or cones on each side of the tooth, making double processes thickly enamelled on the cones or masticating surface.

The maxilla inferior was in two parts naturally, teeth the same as in the maxilla superior, and from the appearance of both jaws, I concluded they had their full complement of teeth—(I judged the head to which these bones belonged was small, as I had teeth of the same kind more than 5 times the size of the largest of either jaw—each under-jaw with the teeth weighing 48 lbs.)

I had a number of teeth ribbed transversely on the masticating surface, and enamelled, weighing from 1½ to 12 lbs. each.

Of the teeth of the mammoth kind furnished with double-coned or blunt-pointed processes on the masticating surface and thickly enamelled and generally 4 processes for insertion in the jaw, as many as a wagon and 4 horses could draw, weighing from 12 to 20 lbs. each.

One small femoris, weight 31 lbs.; 4 ribs, weight and length not recollected—they appeared to be so connected with the vertebrae as to throw their edge outwards; one tusk weighing 100 lbs., 21 inches in circumference, and measuring 10 ft. 6 in. in length; its form thus—one horn 5 ft. long, weight 21 lbs.

The bones of one paw nearly filled a flour barrel; it had 4 claws and then the bones were regularly placed together measured from the os calcis to the end of either middle claw 5 feet 2 inches.

The bones of this paw were similar to those of a bear's foot. Where I found these bones, I found large quantities of bears bones at the same time, and had an opportunity of arranging and comparing the bones together, and the similarity was striking in everything particular except size.

The vertebrae of the back and neck, when arranged in order with the os sacrum and coecygis, measured nearly 60 feet, allowing for cartilages. Though I am not confident the bones all belonged to one animal, and the number of vertebrae I cannot recollect.

I had some thigh bone of incognita of a monstrous size when compared with my other bones, which I much regret I neither weighed or measured, and a number of large bones so much impaired by time it was fruitless to conjecture to what part of any animal they belonged.

As to the probability of obtaining some more bones, and the method of attempting it; the best answer I can give will be a relation how and where I procured the fore-mentioned: They were all procured at a place, called the Big Bone Lick, about 60 miles [by river] below this place and 3 from the Ohio. From my long residence in this country I had long cherished a desire to make researches at Big Bone Lick, but my circumstances (having a large family, and my practice as a physician, though extensive, is not profitable, owing to the poverty of the people) would not enable me to bear the necessary expenses. About 3 years ago, some persons understanding the avidity with which skeletons of this kind were sought after in Europe, and believing a complete skeleton of the mammoth might be procured, said that it would sell well in Europe. After several exertions to obtain what might be necessary to carry my object into execution, I accordingly proceeded to Big Bone Lick, and with a few hands, such as my trifling resources would permit, commenced my researches, when the agent of David Ross of Virginia (who owns the tract of land), forbid my proceeding further. Since which time I have endeavored, by every means which my contracted situation enables me, to procure liberty to prosecute my search.

Big Bone Lick was formerly a salt marsh—Salt is made there at present—we generally dug through several layers of small bones, in a stiff blue clay, such as deer; elk; buffalo and bear bone, in great numbers, many of them much broken, below which was a strata of gravel and salt water, in which we found the large bones, some nearly 11 feet deep in the ground though they were found upon the surface.

The large bones were not found regularly connected together as those of a carcase, which has been consumed by time without disturbance, and I was led to form strong suspicions, that the carcase of the large animals were preyed upon and the bones scattered here and there.—I am so firmly persuaded that large—nay, almost any quantity of teeth bones and tusks may be procured,—that I have long entertained a sanguine hope of bettering my circumstances by procuring skeletons, provided I could obtain permission to prosecute my search, perhaps it may be in the power of your learned body to procure me this permission, and if the society would wish collections of the bones of these nondescripts for their own use, I would undertake to superintend the collection and forward it to Philadelphia, or elsewhere, for such compensation as the Society should think proper to allow me for my trouble and quitting my business during the time of the work. I spent about 4 weeks in my former research, with 6 and sometimes 8 hands, and I think with 10 or 12 hands (who must be found, victuals, and liquor), I could completely search the whole Lick. The expense would be about $1.25 each man per day; we could take provisions from this town, or take a hunter to kill for us. I have now, respected sir, given all the information that suggests itself, and have mentioned the place where the collection is to be made, and the best method to pursue. With sincere wishes, that the Society may prosper, and that you may long continue your labors for the benefit of your country, I am,

With sincere respect, your friend,

WILLIAM GOFORTH.

THE JEFFERSONIAN ERA

IV

The Jeffersonian Era

"Neither mammoth nor elephant, but a distinct kind—a mastodon."

No time was lost by Mr. Jefferson after having received Dr. Goforth's letter. The President had known David Ross, owner of Big Bone Lick, for a number of years. He immediately wrote him for permission to make fossil excavations near the celebrated springs in northern Kentucky. At the same time he perfected arrangements for Captain William Clark, who had returned from the far West on his famous expedition with Captain Lewis, to go to Big Bone and make the collection for him. In the late winter of 1807, he wrote Dr. Wistar of Philadelphia the following letter[1] requesting a list of the bones desired to complete the fossil collection of the American Philosophical Society.

Washington, February 25, 1807

To Dr. Caspar Wistar:
Dear Sir:

I enclose you a letter from Dr. Goforth on the subject of the bones of the mammoth. Immediately on the receipt of this, as I found it was in my power to accomplish the wishes of the society for the completion of this skeleton with more certainty than through the channel proposed in the letter, I set the thing into motion, so that it will be effected without any expense to the society, or trouble other than to indicate the particular bones wanting. Being acquainted with

---

[1] *The Writings of Thomas Jefferson.* Vol. XI, pp. 158, 159, 308. Washington, 1904.

Mr. Ross, proprietor of the Big Bone Lick, I wrote to him for permission to search for such particular bones as the society might desire, and I expect to receive it in a few days. Captain Clarke[2] (companion of Captain Lewis) who is now here, agrees, as he passes through that country, to stop at the Lick, employ laborers, and superintend the search at my expense, not that of the society, and to send me the specific bones wanted, without further trespassing on the deposit, about which Mr. Ross would be tender, and particularly where he apprehended that the person employed would wish to collect for himself. If, therefore, you will be so good as to send me a list of the bones wanting (the one you formerly sent me having been forwarded to Dr. Brown), the business shall be effected without encroaching at all on the funds of the society, and it will be particularly gratifying to me to have the opportunity of being of some use to them. But send me the list if you please without any delay, as Captain Clarke returns in a few days, and we should lose the opportunity. I send you a paper from Dr. Thornton for the society. Accept my friendly salutations and assurances of great esteem and respect.

THOMAS JEFFERSON

Evidently this large scale collecting of mammal fossils for President Jefferson at Big Bone Lick proceeded satisfactorily for we find him, in December, noting completion of the work in Kentucky and sending General Clark his thanks for the service he rendered. This letter also reveals the President's desire for a wide variety of these "Big Bones" to have been really keen for, although Clark had sent him a very "considerable" collection, he is at some pains to have the General send him some additional bones he had recovered and stored

---

[2] President Jefferson, it will be noted, usually mispelled Captain Clark's name with a final e—Clarke.

with his brother, General George Rogers Clark, at Clarksville. Jefferson's letters to both of the Clarks in regard to these fossils follow:

Washington, December 19, 1807.

General William Clarke,[3]

Dear Sir,—I have duly received your two favors of September 20th, and November 10th, and am greatly obliged, indeed, by the trouble you have been so good as to take in procuring for me as thorough a supplement to the bones of the Mammoth as can now be had. I expect daily to receive your bill for all the expenses, which shall be honored with thanks.

The collection you have made is so considerable that it has suggested an idea I had not before. I see that after taking out for the Philosophical Society everything they shall desire, there will remain such a collection of duplicates as will be a grateful offering from me to the National Institute of France, for whom I am bound to do something. But in order to make it more considerable, I find myself obliged to ask the addition of those which you say you have deposited with your brother at Clarkesville, such as ribs, backbones, leg bones, thigh bones, ham hips, shoulder-blades, parts of the upper and under jaw, teeth of the Mammoth and Elephant, and parts of the Mammoth tusks, to be forwarded hereafter, if necessary.

I avail myself of these last words to ask that they may be packed and forwarded to me by the way of New Orleans, as the others have been. I do this with the less hesitation, knowing these things can be of little value to yourself or brother, so much in the way of furnishing yourselves, if desired, and because I know they will be so acceptable to

---

[3] *The Writings of Thomas Jefferson.* Vol. XI, pp. 404-405. Washington, D. C., 1904.

an institution to which, as a member, I wish to be of some use. I salute you with great friendship and respect.

THOMAS JEFFERSON

Washington, December 19, 1807.

General George Rogers Clarke,[4]

Dear General,—As I think it probable your brother will have left you before the enclosed comes to hand, I have left it open, and request you to read it, and do for me what it asks of him, and what he will do should he still be with you, that is to say to have the bones packed and forwarded for me to William Brown, collector at New Orleans, who will send them on to me.

I avail myself of this occasion of recalling myself to your memory, and of assuring you that time has not lessened my friendship for you. We are both now grown old. You have been enjoying in retirement the recollections of the services you have rendered your country, and I am about to retire without an equal consciousness that I have not occupied places in which others would have done more good. But in all places and times I shall wish you every happiness, and salute you with great friendship and esteem.

THOMAS JEFFERSON

And, at the same time, anticipating shortly the arrival of the fossils themselves, he penned a letter to Dr. Wistar in Philadelphia, outlining generally what the Clark collection would contain, and suggesting that the doctor come to Washington and be his guest for a week so that they might carefully examine the collection. Suggesting that he wished to send some portion of these bones to the National Institute of

---

The Writings of Thomas Jefferson. Vol. XI, p. 406. Washington, D. C., 1904.

France, in Paris, he enumerated the attractions of Washington and stated that, in the capitol, "you will see one room especially to which Europe can show nothing superior." His reference was to the room in the White House which he then planned and finally did set aside for General Clark's collection from Big Bone. The letter follows:

Washington, December 19, 1807.

Dr. Caspar Wistar[5]

Dear Sir,—I have lately received a letter from General Clarke. He has employed ten laborers several weeks, at the Big-bone Lick, and has shipped the result, in three large boxes, down the Ohio, via New Orleans, for this place, where they are daily expected. He has sent, 1st, of the Mammoth, as he calls it, frontals, jaw-bones, tusks, teeth, ribs; a thigh, and a leg, and some bones of the paw; 2d, of what he calls the Elephant, a jaw-bone, tusks, teeth, ribs; 3d, of something of the Buffalo species, a head and some other bones unknown. My intention, in having this research thoroughly made, was to procure for this society as complete a supplement to what is already possessed as that Lick can furnish at this day, and to serve them first with whatever they wish to possess of it. There is a tusk and a femur which General Clarke procured particularly at my request, for a special kind of cabinet I have at Monticello.

But the great mass of the collection are mere duplicates of what you possess at Philadelphia, of which I would wish to make a donation to the National Institute of France, which I believe has scarcely any specimens of the remains of these animals. But how to make the selection without the danger of sending away something which might be useful to our own society? Indeed, my friend, you must give a week to

---

[5] *The Writings of Thomas Jefferson,* Vol. XI, pp. 403, 404. Washington, D. C., 1904.

this object. You cannot but have some wish to see Washington for its site, and some of its edifices, which will give you pleasure. You will see one room especially, to which Europe can show nothing superior. Baltimore, too, is an object. Take your lodgings at the tavern close by us. Mess with me every day, and in the intervals of your perlustrations of the city, Navy Yard, Capitol, etc., examine these bones, and set apart what you would wish for the society. I will give you notice when they arrive here, and then you will select a time when you can best absent yourself for a week from Philadelphia. I hope you will not deny us this great service, and I salute you with friendship and respect.

THOMAS JEFFERSON

Finally, in 1808, when national interest had reached the flashing point of excitement over the embargo, and his policy was under the most severe denunciation by his opponents, Jefferson at last came into possession of the consignment of "big bones" sent to him by General Clark from Kentucky. Seeking relief from pressing affairs of State, he directed that some 300 specimens or more be unboxed and arranged by themselves in a room in the White House,[6] as he had planned for over a year. Here he found rest and relaxation in quiet paleontological studies of the amazing relics of the glacial age that had been preserved in the salty bog at Big Bone Lick. Again he urged Dr. Wistar to come, "satisfy your curiosity" and "take your breakfast and dinner with us." It is to be presumed that the amiable physician quit his abode in the Quaker City on receipt of invitation from the President, and made his way directly to Washington. What times these two great men had in measuring and marking this fine collection

---

[6] *Contributions to the History of American Geology.* George P. Merrill, p. 213 in Report of National Museum. Washington, 1904.

BIG BONE LICK 53

we may infer from the tone of another Jefferson letter. As this historic conference advanced day by day it may be said to have actually ushered in the beginning of American governmental work in Paleontology[7] with fossils from Big Bone Lick.

Jefferson wrote:

Washington, March 20, 1808.

Doctor Caspar Wistar,[8]

Dear Sir,—Yours of the 12th is received. Congress, I think, will rise in about three weeks,—say about the 11th of April, and I shall leave this place five or six days after, on a visit of some length to Monticello. This illy accords with your journey to the westward in May; but can you not separate your excursion to this place from the western journey? Between Philadelphia and this place is but two days, and the roads are already fine. I would propose, therefore, that you should come a few days before Congress rises, so as to satisfy that article of your curiosity. The bones are spread in a large room, where you can work at your leisure, undisturbed by any mortal, from morning till night, taking your breakfast and dinner with us. It is a precious collection, consisting of upwards of three hundred bones, few of them of the large kinds which are already possessed. There are four pieces of the head, one very clear, and distinctly presenting the whole face of the animal. The height of his forehead is most remarkable. In this figure, the indenture at the eye gives a prominence of six inches to the forehead. There are four jaw-bones tolerably entire, with several teeth in them, and some fragments; three tusks like elephants; one ditto totally different, the

---

[7] *Jefferson As a Man of Science.* Cyrus Adler, pp. III-X, Vol. XIX, Writings of Thomas Jefferson, Washington, 1904.

[8] *The Writings of Thomas Jefferson.* Vol. XII, pp. 15-16. Washington, 1904.

largest probably ever seen, being now from nine to ten feet long, though broken off at both ends; some ribs; an abundance of teeth studded and also of those of the striated or ribbed kind; a fore leg complete; and then about two hundred small bones, chiefly of the foot. This is probably the most valuable part of the collection, for General Clarke, aware that we had specimens of the larger bones, has gathered up everything of the small kind. There is one horn of a colossal animal. The bones which came do not correspond exactly with General Clarke's description; probably there were some omissions of his packers. Having sent my books to Monticello, I have nothing here to assist you but the "Encyclopedie Methodique." I hope you will make this a separate excursion; and come before Congress rises, whenever it best suits you. I salute you with friendship and respect.

THOMAS JEFFERSON.

Jefferson's deep interest in the fossils recovered from Big Bone Lick is evidenced by his third letter written over a year later when the second consignment of bones sent by General Clark from Clarksville on the Ohio did not arrive promptly. This letter also indicates that he sent part of the previous collection to the National Institute of France in Paris:

Monticello, September 10, 1809.

General William Clarke,[9]

Dear General,—Your favor of June 2d came duly to hand in July, and brought me a repetition of the proofs of your kindness to me........ The three boxes of bones which you had been so kind as to send to New Orleans for me, as mentioned in your letter of June 2d, arrived there safely,

---

[9] *The Writings of Thomas Jefferson.* Vol. XII, pp. 309-311. Washington, 1904.

and were carefully shipped by the collector, and the bill of lading sent to me. But the vessel put into the Havana, under embargo distress, was there condemned as unseaworthy, and her enrollment surrendered at St. Mary's. What was done with my three boxes I have not learned but have written to Mr. Brown, the collector, to have inquiry made after them. The bones of this animal are now in such a state of evanescence as to render it important to save what we can of them. Of those you had formerly sent me, I reserved a very few for myself; I got Dr. Wistar to select from the rest every piece which could be interesting to the Philosophical Society, and sent the residue to the National Institute of France.

These have enabled them to decide that the animal was neither a mammoth nor an elephant, but of a distinct kind, to which they have given the name of Mastodon, from the protuberance of its teeth. These, from their forms, and the immense mass of their jaws, satisfy me this animal must have been arboriverous. Nature seems not to have provided other food sufficient for him, and the limb of a tree would be no more to him than a bough of a cotton tree to a horse. You mention in your letter that you are proceeding with your family to Fort Massac. This informs me that you have a family, and I sincerely congratulate you on it, while some may think it will render you less active in the service of the world, those who take a sincere interest in your personal happiness, and who know that, by a law of our nature, we cannot be happy without the endearing connections of a family, will rejoice for your sake as I do. This world has, of right, no further claims on yourself and General Lewis, but such as you may voluntarily render according to your convenience, or as they may make it your interest. I wrote lately to the Governor, but be so good as to repeat my affectionate attachments to him, and be assured of the same to yourself, with every sentiment of esteem and respect.

THOMAS JEFFERSON

It is thus apparent that the work of collecting[10] done by General William Clark at Big Bone for the President beginning in 1807 bore much fruit. Mr. Jefferson, paying for the field work personally, took the great fossils to the White House and thus endowed them with popular interest. Finally he gave them to two of the leading museums of the day, the American Philosophical Society in Philadelphia and the National Institute of France, in Paris. The finest specimen recovered as a result of this research was a skull of the great arctic musk ox *Bootherium*. It is the only one that has ever been taken from this fossil locality. This fossil, of course, remained in that portion of the collection that was presented by Mr. Jefferson to the American Philosophical Society, of which he was then the president. It is now the property of the Academy of Natural Sciences of Philadelphia.

[10] *Writings of Thomas Jefferson.* Vol. XI, pp. 158-159, 403-404, and 406, also Vol. XII, pp. 15-16. Washington, 1904.

LATER AND RECENT COLLECTORS

V

Later and Recent Collectors

"That knocks Moses."

The physical appearance of Big Bone Lick during the early part of the nineteenth century gradually lost its primeval aspect. Each party visiting the lick stripped it of whatever fossils they could find and carry away. Most of these collections, due to the hazards of the journey and the times, were lost. A few escaped destruction and came to enrich private collections in America and public displays in England and on the Continent. In time all of the lick-strewn fossils disappeared. The last of the great bones were removed from the surface surrounding these famous northern Kentucky salt springs, about the time General William Clark made his extensive collection for President Thomas Jefferson. This final clean-up was made by a number of avid collectors who dispatched them to widely separated parts of the United States and Europe, as a purely commercial pursuit.

It is recorded that one collection from Big Bone sold for $5,000.00 and others, depending upon their size and importance, at similar figures.[1] Since these early times a very considerable number of bones, exhibiting a representative Pleistocene mammalian fauna—much of it with a decidedly arctic characteristic—have been exhumed from the salty muds and marls of this famous old bog. Marked as the greatest depository of proboscidian bones in America, it has widely

---

[1] *History of Kentucky.* Lewis Collins, pp. 180-181. Maysville, 1850.

received and well deserves the name of the *graveyard of the Mammoth.*

Towards the latter part of the first quarter of the nineteenth century erosion about the lick invited further investigation and, in 1816 or 1817, John D. Clifford, of Lexington, visited Big Bone and exhumed numerous fossils which he removed to his cabinet in the heart of the Bluegrass country. Among these were the tusks of a mastodon and some horns of the extinct oxen. Later, after Clifford's death, this unique Lexington collection, including his megalonyx material from White Cave, was purchased and removed to the museum in Cincinnati, from whence, following the purchase by John Price Wetherill in 1829, it was shipped East and became the property of the Academy of Natural Science in Philadelphia. In 1819 a considerable collection of big bones was made for the Western Museum Society of Cincinnati. Two years later, in 1821, the eccentric professor of natural history at Transylvania, Constantine S. Rafinesque,[2] visited Big Bone Lick, but was prevented from making any fossil collection by the owner, whom Rafinesque has described as a surly man who thought digging would take the water away from his springs. In the summer of 1828 William Cooper,[3] in company with Mr. I. Cozzens,[*] of New York, made a journey to the lick, caused several excavations to be made and, to use his own words,

---

[2] *Visit to Big Bone Lick in 1821.* C. A. Rafinesque, Month. Am. Jour. Geol. Vol. I, p. 355. February, 1832.

[3] *Notices of Big Bone Lick.* William Cooper, Month. Am. Jour. of Geol., Vol. I, No. 4, pp. 158-174. October, 1831.

[*] He produced two MSS. maps of Big Bone Lick, one in 1828 and another in 1830. Each of these original MSS. maps are in the archives of the New York Historical Society. Photostat copies of each are possessed by the Filson Club, the Kentucky State Historical Society, and the writer.

"collected everything that seemed likely to add to our store of information concerning the place."

In 1830 still another collection, and a large one, was made by Captain Benjamin Finnell, who resided at that time at the licks. He conveyed his finds to a Mr. Graves who dispersed them to a number of museum purchasers in the eastern United States and England. This so encouraged Mr. William Bullock, of Kentucky, that he followed Mr. Finnell and was richly rewarded for his labors in excavating about the licks. Such wide distribution of giant bones taken from this remarkable northern Kentucky lick soon gave it great pre-eminence in the scientific world. As discussions increased concerning it, famous personalities and scientific travellers made it a mecca and visitors began to be drawn to it from various parts of the civilized world.

The distinguished early American scientist, Benjamin Silliman of Yale College, after viewing, in New York City, a fine collection of Big Bone Lick fossils, one that contained twenty-two tusks and one skull, that alone weighed 5,300 pounds, said, in substance, that they produced in the beholder the strongest conviction that races of animals of vast magnitude formerly existed in this country. These beasts, he asserted, also had been very numerous; and the Mastodon, at least, probably ranged in herds over the entire American continent. In the American Journal of Science, in 1831, he wrote:[4]

> It is stated by the person who exhibits this collection, that the skull, and the tusks which it contains, weigh upward of five hundred pounds; that a pair of tusks now lying in

---

[4] *(Remarks Relative to Big Bone Lick Fossils.)* Benjamin Silliman, Am. Jour. Science, Vol. XX, pp. 371-372. New Haven, 1831.

the room, and supposed to belong to the same species, weighed six hundred pounds when taken from the ground.

During the same year that famous trio of paleontologists—W. Cooper, J. A. Smith, and J. E. DeKay,[5] also wrote on these Big Bone relics as did Rafinesque and numerous others. The great English geologist, Sir Charles Lyell,[6] visited this notable Kentucky fossil locality during his American travels in 1841 and 1842, and described it soon thereafter. Joseph Leidy[7] began a series of descriptions of its fauna in 1847, and David Dale Owen, Kentucky's eminent State Geologist, visited the locality a few years before the ravages of Civil War caused scientific investigations in the middle Ohio valley to be temporarily laid aside. Some gauge of the wide interest awakened in the "Big Bones" of this Kentucky lick, during the first half of the nineteenth century, may be seen in the fact that this lick found inclusion in the indexes of all the principal geological, paleontological, and scientific journals and books of America, England, Germany, and France.

In 1868 Nathaniel Southgate Shaler,[8] a native of Newport, Kentucky, and, some years later, the Dean of the Lawrence Scientific School at Harvard, came to Big Bone Lick determined "that these licks should be worked to their very bottom in search of their possible contents." After extensive exca-

---

[5] *Report to the Lyceum of Natural History on a Collection of Fossil Bones Disinterred at Big Bone Lick, Kentucky, etc.:* W. Cooper, J. A. Smith, and J. E. DeKay, Am. Jour. Science, Vol. XX, pp. 370-372. New York, 1831.

[6] *Travels in North America, 1841-1842.* Charles Lyell, Murray ed. Vol. II, pp. 62-66. New York, 1845.

[7] *On the Fossil Horse of America.* Joseph Leidy, Proc. Acad. Nat. Sci., Phila., Vol. III, p. 263. 1847.

[8] *(Big Bone Lick.)* Reports of Progress, Ky. Geol. Survey; Series II, Vol. III, Chapter III, pp. 66-69 and p. 197. Frankfort, 1877.

vations and collecting he developed a distinct order[9] of succession beginning with *Elephas primigenius*—the glacial or hairy mammoth—at eight feet below the surface. With it occurred *Bootherium*, the arctic musk ox. Above these great Pleistocene giants of the plains and tundra, he found *Mastodon Ohioticus*, then, above that, a horse—probably *Equus-complicatus*. And above this the caribou and the elk. At or close to the surface he found the buffalo, the bear, and the deer, the superior position of whose bones proved beyond doubt that they were late comers into the region and probably did not encounter the other great beasts of the glacial age. Professor Shaler's deductions, following these excavations, were that both of the great Pleistocene elephants—the mammoth and the mastodon—"survived the closure of the main glacial action for a very long time—and may have continued down to a relatively recent time."

Coincidental with Professor Shaler's efforts to unravel the history of accession of the various mammals at Big Bone Lick in the mid-summer of 1868, a certain amount of digging in proximity of one of the saline springs was undertaken to improve the facilities for the barreling of the water to be sold. In doing this it is recorded that on August 1st, a wagon load of bones of the mammoth was discovered within a space of about fifteen feet. Among these was a tusk ten inches thick and twelve feet long, a portion of the backbone or joined vertebrae of about equal dimensions, and a tooth fifteen inches long, six inches thick, weighing about twenty pounds.[10] It is not known now where these impressive fossils were finally

---
[9] *On the Age of the Bison in the Ohio Valley*. N. S. Shaler, Memoir, Vol. I, Part II, pp. 232-236. Cambridge, 1876.

[10] *History of Kentucky*. Richard Collins, Vol. I, pp. 191-192. Covington, 1882.

deposited or whether they were ever given the immediate care required for their preservation or not. Possibly they were allowed to slowly fall into ruins and become a total loss to science, as have so many other fine collections taken from Big Bone Lick. Certainly today such a discovery would be widely heralded, and public opinion, supported by common sense and good judgment, would direct that all bones recovered be adequately preserved in the interest of the public good.

A few years ago an intimate friend of Dean Shaler, writing of the excavations for Pleistocene fossils made by this celebrated geologist at Big Bone Lick, said:[11]

From a scientific point of view one of the most interesting episodes of this time was the unearthing of the fossil remains of [the glacial] elephants at Big Bone Lick. Mr. Shaler was anxious to acquire these specimens for the Museum [at Harvard University], and with this end in view he tried to get its friends to subscribe money for carrying on the excavations. But while the treasurer earnestly desired to enrich the Museum by these possessions, money was short. Finally the owner of the thirty acres of bones [at the lick] gave Mr. Shaler permission to dig at pleasure. One of the tusks unearthed was eleven feet long on the curve. It may be mentioned here that these bones, which at first could find no purchasers, were later sold by the pound. Mr. Shaler told some amusing stories of the "natives" who sat on the periphery of the excavations silently watching all that was going on. One in particular referred to an old man who had been constant in attendance. At last one day when the fragments of a huge elephant were dug out, he exclaimed, "That knocks Moses," and, in a disgusted frame of mind, walked away, never to return.

The largest of the present-day foreign collections from Big Bone Lick is that housed in the museum of the Royal

---

[11] *The Autobiography of Nathaniel Southgate Shaler.* Pp. 247-248. Boston, 1909.

College of Surgeons at Lincoln's Inn Fields in London, England. This great fossil assemblage contains some seventy-five separate specimens and is confined entirely to the mastodon and the mammoth. All of these proboscidian bones have been indexed; but few, if any, have been described. The catalogue,[12] involving this collection, according to the letter of R. H. Burne of November 22, 1927, states:

Of the bones and teeth of the Mammoth and Mastodon from the neighborhood of the River Ohio, some were purchased at the sale of Mr. Bullock's collection in 1820, and others at that of Mr. Hyhan's in 1836. The latter are stated in the sale catalogue to have been found 22 feet below the surface of Big Bone Lick in Boone County, State of Kentucky, in the autumn of 1830 and dug up by Capt. Benjamin Finnell and others .... The specimens from the two collections are not distinguished in the old catalogue, but some of them are labelled "Bullock's Collection." The Hunterian specimens, as suggested by Mr. Burne, must date before 1792. One of them is marked as having been sent by Dr. Caspar Wistar of Philadelphia. This British collection contains the following complete and fragmentary bones:

Elephas primigenius. tusks 4, skulls 2, mandible 1, molars 5.
Mastodon americanus. mandibles 8, tusks 5, molars 16, atlas vertebrae 3, cervical vertebra 1, mscl. vertebrae 2, Sacrum 2, ribs 1, sternun 1, humeri 3, ulna 1, cuneiforme 1, metacarpals 4, innominates 3, femurs 4, patella 1, tibiae 3, astragalus 1, calcis 1.

The British Museum with a remarkable collection of about twenty-five specimens, many of which are of the first order of

---

[12] Catalogue of Osteology and Dentition of Vertebrated Animals, Recent and Extinct. Part II, Mammalia by W. H. Flower, p. 465. London, 1884.

importance from a paleontological standpoint, adds greatly to the distinction of London as a depository of Big Bone Lick fossils. Richard Lydekker has provided this list in his catalogues:[13]

> 40847. Fragment of the right ramus of a mandible, probably belonging to the present species; from the Pleistocene of Big-Bone Lick, Kentucky, U. S. A. Gift, C. Falconer, Esq., 1867.
>
> 342. The right half of the palate, with $m.3$; from "Big-Bone-Lick." Purchased. About 1836.
>
> M.146. Fragment of the left maxilla, with $m.1$; from "Big-Bone-Lick." Purchased, 1882. Enniskillen Collection.
>
> 335. The germ of the second right upper true molar; from "Big-Bone Lick." Purchased. About 1836.
>
> 336. The second right upper true molar, in a more worn condition; from "Big-Bone-Lick." Purchased. About 1836.
>
> M.380. The second right upper true molar, in a similar stage of wear; from "Big-Bone-Lick." Egerton Collection. Purchased 1882.
>
> 7439. The second right upper true molar, in a similar stage of wear; from "Big-Bone-Lick." Mantell Collection. Purchased 1836.
>
> 13 (O.C.) The second right upper true molar, in a much-worn condition; from "Big-Bone-Lick."
>
> M.451. The second left upper true molar, from "Big-Bone-Lick." Enniskillen Collection. Purchased, 1882.

---

[13] Richard Lydekker. Catalogue of the Fossil Mammalia in the British Museum (Natural History), Pt. II, p. 27, 1885; Pt. IV, pp. 17-25, 1886.

M.451. a. The third right upper true molar (Imperfect): from "Big-Bone-Lick." This tooth agrees in character with No. 17326. Enniskillen Collection. Purchased, 1882.

343. The left ramus of the mandible, with m.2 and m.3; from "Big-Bone-Lick." Figured by Falconer and Cautley in the "Fauna Antiqua Sivalensis." pl. XXXV. figs. 4, 5.

M.147. Part of the left ramus of the mandible, with m.1 and m.2; from "Big-Bone-Lick." Enniskillen Collection. Purchased, 1882.

40786. The second right lower milk-molar; from "Big-Bone-Lick." Presented by C. Falconer, Esq. 1867.

M.2850. The second right lower true molar, almost unworn; from "Big-Bone-Lick." Presented by Prof. Sir R. Owen, K. C. B. 1859.

M.150. The unworn second left lower true molar; from "Big-Bone-Lick." Enniskillen Collection. Purchased, 1882.

337. The second left lower true molar, in a half-worn condition; from "Big-Bone-Lick." Enniskillen Collection. Purchased, 1882.

40782. The second left lower true molar; from "Big-Bone-Lick." Presented by C. Falconer, Esq. 1867.

338. The third right lower true molar; from "Big-Bone-Lick." Purchased.

339. The third right lower true molar; from "Big-Bone-Lick." The talon is small. Purchased.

340. The third left lower true molar; from "Big-Bone-Lick." The talon is double, and of large size. Purchased.

341. The third left lower true molar; from "Big-Bone-Lick." Purchased.

7435. The almost unworn third right lower true molar, bisected in a longitudinal and horizontal plane at the base of the crown; from "Big-Bone-Lick." Mantell Collection. Purchased, 1836.

344. The glenoidal part of the right scapula; from "Big-Bone-Lick." Purchased.

41661. A lumbar vertebra; from "Big-Bone-Lick." Toulmin-Smith Collection. Purchased, 1869.

The most important of the American collections from Big Bone Lick is that found in the Museum of Comparative Zoology at Harvard College, Cambridge, Massachusetts. This priceless assemblage of mammalian fossils was collected by Professor Shaler in 1868 and is significant because of its representative character. About fifteen separate species are indicated in the following list which was prepared by Alfred S. Romer:

Bison bison: Skulls 4, pt. skull 7, maxillae 10, nasals 3, premaxillae 10, otic region 1, horn core 1, lower jaws 23, fragments do. 8, teeth 102, hyoids 3, vertebral column 1, atlas 10, axis 13, cervical vertebrae 65, dorsal vertebrae 206, lumbar vertebrae 52, sacrum 17, caudal 7, ribs 387, pieces of sternum 7, scapula 20, humerus 12, radius 6, ulna 6, pelvis 32, femur 27, tibia 36, patella 8, scaphoid 6, lumar 7, magnum 10, cuboid plus navicular 20, cuneiform 4, unciform 3, calcaneum 62, astragalus 40, sesamoid bones 9, metacarpals 65, metatarsals 43, phalanges 102, misc. fgts. 7.

Bison latifrons: Molars 8.

Bison indet: Fragments 6.

BIG BONE LICK 69

Equus complicatus: Molars 3; *Equus sp.* phalanges 2.
Rangifer tarandus: Pieces antler 16, metatarsal 1.
Ovibos or *Boofrons:* Vertebrae 8, metatarsal 1.
Cervus canadensis: Antlers 3, teeth 3.
Odocoileus virginianus: Antlers 4, metatarsals 2.
Cervalces? (entered as "Megaceros?"): Humerus 1, femur 1, tibia 1.
Deer, indet: Ribs 3.
Alces machlis: Molar 1.
Dicotyles? Part humerus 1.
Ursus sp: Part humerus 1.
Mylodon or *Megalonyx:* Unguals 3.
Elephas sp: Neural spine 1, pelvis 3, metacarpals 2.
Elephas columbi: Molar 1.
Elephas americanus: Teeth 4.
Mastodon americanus: Teeth 14.
Mastodon? Fgts. ribs 5.
Mastodon or *Elephas:* Fgts. of tusks 4, vertebra 1, neural spine 1, fgts. ribs 5, sacrals 4, fibula 1, patella 1, trapezium 1, calcaneum 2, metacarpal 1, metatarsals 2.
Unidentified: 5.

The largest publicly-owned collection of fossils from Big Bone Lick in this Commonwealth at the present time is found in the Museum of Geology at the University of Kentucky in Lexington. This collection, though not great, is typical since it exhibits representatives of the mammoth, the mastodon, the horse, and the bison. A number of these specimens were collected by the author for the Kentucky Geological Survey in 1924. The following list was prepared and enclosed in his letter of August 23, 1935, by Prof. David M. Young, Curator of the Museum:

No. 1. Tooth of Mammoth (Elephas columbi?). Collected by Dr. Willard Rouse Jillson.

No. 2. Skull of Bison (Bison occidentalis). Collected by Dr. Jillson.

No. 3. Vertebra of Mastodon (Mammut americanum). Collected by Prof. A. M. Miller.

No. 4. Bones of Mastodon (Mammut americanum). (Probably pelvic.) Collected by Dr. Jillson.

No. 5. Tusk of Mammoth or Mastodon (Elephas or Mammut-Fragmentary). Collected by Dr. Jillson.

No. 6. Teeth of Horse (Equus complicatus). Collected by Archaeological Museum.

Another important, but small, group of specimens from Big Bone Lick is displayed by The Filson Club in its museum in Louisville, Kentucky. These items, collected by Mr. R. C. B. Thruston on May 6, 1932, and recently exhibited to the writer, consist of the following:

No. 1. Tusk of Mastodon, immature individual, 3 fragments.

No. 2. Tooth (molar) of Mammoth, immature individual, 2 fragments.

Another small but interesting Big Bone collection is to be found in Louisville in the city museum located in the basement of the Public Library. It consists of the following two specimens according to Lucien Beckner:

No. 1. Elephas columbi?: tusk 9x5½ inches, in very bad condition.

No. 2. Mastodon americanus: lower jaw, 6x2½ inches.

A private collection of mammal fossils taken from Big Bone Lick is owned by Mr. J. B. Moore, who, for many

BIG BONE LICK 71

years, has been a resident of the hamlet of Big Bone. The president of the Big Bone Lick Association has been advised that these fossils will be given to the association for public display whenever it provides proper housing for them on the grounds surrounding the licks from which they were exhumed. This private collection, according to Mr. Moore, contains individual bones of the mammoth, mastodon, and bison.

One of the most interesting American collections—because it is probably the earliest now extant—taken from Big Bone Lick is that of the Academy of Natural Science of Philadelphia. This collection is sufficiently representative to be notable in its own right since it exhibits fossil bones from at least nine separate Pleistocene and Recent species and many more individuals. Here are found the horse, the tapir, the elk, the buffalo, the musk ox, the mammoth, and the mastodon. Paleontologists will always feel particular warmth toward this group of Kentucky glacial fossils because some of the specimens were collected at Big Bone by General William Clark, at the instance of Thomas Jefferson, and were later given by the President, after he had examined them in the White House, to the American Philosophical Society which, in turn, bequeathed them to the Academy. The list of these unique fossils as prepared and submitted by J. Percey Moore, Secretary, follows:

11454–57 Equus americanus, Leidy (Horse) leg and toe bones.
11496 Equus sp. 11 molar teeth.
11504 Tapirus haysii Leidy (Tapir) 1 molar.
11567–72–74 Cervus americanus, Harlan (Elk) 2 foot bones, end of femur, ankle bones.

12966	Bison sp. (Buffalo) many leg bones, parts of skull, etc.
12990	Bison antiquus Leidy, horn cone (original type specimen).
12993	Bison latifrons, Leidy, horn cone and base of skull (original type specimen).
13000	Ovibos cavifrons, Leidy (Musk Ox) right metacarpal.
13056–66	Elephas primigenius (Mammoth) molar teeth.
13126–61	Elephas primigenius molar teeth.
13253	Mastodon americanus (Mastodon) molar.
13306–16	Mastodon americanus Molars and parts of jaws and leg bones.

A small but valuable group of fossils from Big Bone Lick is to be seen in the Museum of Natural History at the University of Rochester in New York State. These bones are catalogued, according to the letter of Lorene C. Karleskind of September 5, 1935, as follows:

No. 1. Mastodon americanus—upper left, last molar (O. P. Hay).
No. 2. Mastodon gigantenus—thoracic (dorsal) vertebra.
No. 3. Equus (complicatus)—metatarsal.
No. 4. Equus (?)—humerus.
No. 5. Equus (?)—hoof phalanx.

In the American Museum of Natural History in New York City, Dr. Barnum Brown states in his letter of July 19, 1935, that there are catalogued only two specimens from Big Bone Lick. These are:

No. 983. Mastodon americanus, last molar.

No. 984. Mastodon americanus, second molar.

The United States National Museum, Smithsonian Institution, in Washington, D. C., unfortunately, has very little original material from Big Bone Lick, according to the letter of W. de C. Ravenel of November 17, 1927. This museum's catalogue gives:

No. 310. A fragment of bone from Big Bone Lick, and elsewhere it cites:

No. 823. A right ramus (cast) of Megalonyx.

No. 824. Upper molar tooth (cast) of Megalonyx.

In the Museum of Natural History, Division of Vertebrate Paleontology of Princeton University at Princeton, New Jersey, the following fossils from Big Bone Lick are on exhibition according to the letter of Glenn L. Jepsen of January 9, 1936:

No. 10314. Bison, jaws, back of skull, and atlas.

Besides the collections indicated above as originating at Big Bone Lick, the writer is certain that there are numerous other, probably small, collections some of which are private, scattered throughout the United States and Canada. Ward's Natural Science Establishment at Rochester, New York, at various times during the past generation or so, secured and distributed many fossils from Big Bone. The exact whereabouts of these fossils is now unknown due to a fire which destroyed the purchase records in Ward's office. Important foreign collections from Big Bone, the detailed description of which it has been impossible to get up to this writing, are believed to exist in Oxford, England, and Paris, France.

ns, deeds
LAND SURVEYS, GRANTS, DEEDS

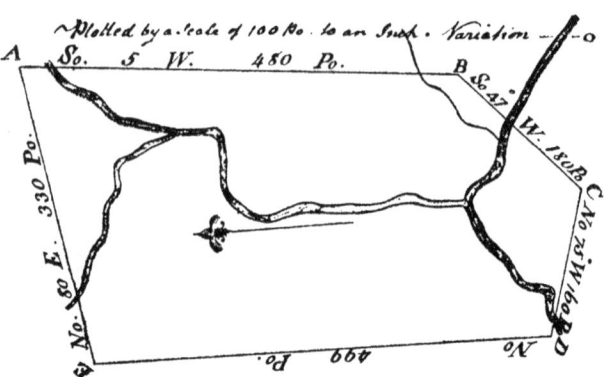

FIRST SURVEY OF BIG BONE LICK
Reduced facsimile of John Floyd's survey of Big Bone Lick and vicinity made for Colonel William Christian, May 12, 1774. Original now in the State Land Office, Frankfort, Kentucky.

VI

Land Surveys, Grants, and Deeds

"Speculation in Kentucky did not always turn out satisfactorily for David Ross."

In the all-but-forgotten journal of early exploration in *Kentucke*, written by Thomas Hanson in 1774, is found the earliest written reference to the first land survey made of Big Bone Lick and the area adjoining. Whether Hanson erred or not in stating that Douglas made this particular survey for Colonel Christian may never be known, but it is certain that the original platted survey itself bears the name of John Floyd, a deputy surveyor under Colonel William Preston, surveyor of Fincastle County, Virginia. In the following transcript[1] of this quaint old land document of 1772, the original of which was discovered and given to the public by the writer in the late spring of 1935, it will be noted there is no mention of the name of James Douglas, who, nevertheless, may have actually run the lines in the field and then turned his work over to Floyd.

DRAWING OF SURVEY

Plotted by a scale of 100 Po. to an inch, Variation O. Surveyed for William Christian 1000 acres of land in Fincastle County (by virtue of the Governor's warrant & agreeable to his Majesty's proclamation of 1763) lying on a South Branch of the Ohio River called the big Bone Creek including the large Buffalo Lick & Salt Spring known by the name of the big Bone Lick being about four miles from the Ohio

[1] Original filed in Virginia Surveys on which grants have been issued. Bundle 94, Kentucky Land Office, Frankfort, Kentucky.

River. Beginning at a large red oak & White Hiccory near the Creek, thence S 5 W 480 Poles to a Sugar Tree & Hiccory Saplin, S 47 W 180 crossing a Branch to a red Oak near a mud lick, N 75 W 160 crossing the great Bone Creek to a Lynn on the hill side, North 499 poles to a Sugar tree & black ash, N 80 E 330 poles to the Beginning.

          Wm. Preston, S. F. C.
No variation   John Floyd, Asst. Surv.
12th May, 1774.

Five years later Thomas Jefferson, then Governor of Virginia, delivered a military grant to Big Bone Lick and its environs to Colonel Christian based on Floyd's 1000 acre survey. Couched in old style colonial English this patent, so different from the matter-of-fact deeds of today, is interesting now because it is the beginning of the present chain of title to the land comprising and surrounding Big Bone Lick. A reproduction of this grant[2] is here appended:

Thomas Jefferson, Esq.
    Governor of the Commonwealth of Virginia.

TO ALL TO WHOM THESE PRESENTS SHALL COME, GREETING;

KNOW YE, That by virtue and in consideration of Military service performed by William Christian in the late war between Great Brittain & France according to the terms of the King of Great Brittains proclamation of 1763;

There is granted by said Commonwealth unto William Christian a certain TRACT OR PARCEL OF LAND, con-

---

[2] *The Kentucky Land Grants.* Willard Rouse Jillson, p. 37, Filson Club Publications No. 33. Louisville, 1925. Recorded in Book 6, page 14, Virginia Grants, Kentucky Land Office, New Capitol, Frankfort, Kentucky.

BIG BONE LICK

taining 1000 acres, by survey, bearing date[3] the [12th] day of [May], one thousand seven hundred and [seventy-four], lying and being in the county of Kentucky on a branch of the Ohio river called the Big bone Creek, including the large Buffaloe lick being about 4 miles from the Ohio river: Beginning at a large red oak and white Hickory near the creek, thence South 5 degrees West 480 poles to a sugartree, and hickory saplin, thence South 47 degrees West 180 poles crossing a branch to a red oak near a mud lick, North 75 degrees West 160 poles crossing the Great Bone Creek to a lyn on the Hill side, North 499 poles to a sugartree and black ash, North 80 degrees East 330 poles to the Beginning, with its appurtenances: TO HAVE AND TO HOLD the said Tract or Parcel of Land, with its appurtenances to the said William Christian, and his heirs forever.

IN WITNESS WHEREOF, the said Thomas Jefferson, Esq., Governor of the Commonwealth of Virginia, hath hereunto set his hand, and caused the lesser Seal of the said Commonwealth to be affixed at Richmond on the 24th day of November, in the year of our Lord one thousand seven hundred and 79 and of the Commonwealth the 4th.

Thirteen months later—December 22, 1780—Colonel Christian, then residing in old Montgomery County, Virginia, sold his 1000-acre grant, including Big Bone Lick, which was described as "the large buffaloe lick," to David Ross of Bedford County. The consideration was "£1350 in specie in hand paid," a goodly sum—about $4455.00—considering the times, for such wild hill and creek lands as these in the then remote and unprotected reaches of northern *Kentucke*. Evidently,

---
[3] Date of survey as shown above was not originally shown in this grant but has been added from Thomas Hanson's journal of 1774. It corresponds exactly, as may be noted, with the date on the original survey by Col. John Floyd.

Christian, the rugged colonial leader of many a bloody encounter with the French and Indians, fully sensed the potential value of the age-old and widely known salt springs at Big Bone, for he drove a good trade. In the economy of a new and growing inland country, essentially without roads, and separated by two great mountain chains—the Blue Ridge and the Alleghenies—from the older settlements along the Atlantic seaboard, he undoubtedly anticipated the added commercial advantage which must come to salt making at Big Bone because of the location of the springs close to the main artery of western trade and travel—the Ohio River. Christian's deed[4] to Ross, in which the old soldier's wife, Anna, joined, is here presented in full because of its interesting construction and phraseology. Its recordation in the old Court of Appeals at Frankfort, together with the affidavits of each of its witnesses, William Dandridge, J. Mosby, John Harvie, and Isham Williams, marked the first sale of land involving Big Bone Lick.

DEED

This Indenture made this twenty second day of December One thousand Seven hundred and Eighty. Between William Christian and Anna his wife of Montgomery County of the one part and David Ross of Bedford County of the other part Witnesseth. William Christian and Anna his wife for and in consideration of the sum of thirteen hundred and fifty pounds specie in hand paid before the sealing and delivery of these presents the receipt whereof they do hereby acknowledge and confess—Have and by these pres-

---

[4] *Old Kentucky Entries and Deeds.* Willard Rouse Jillson, pp. 444, 478, and 526. Filson Club Publications No. 34, Louisville, 1926. Original deed filed in Deed Record Book B, p. 132, Kentucky Court of Appeals, Frankfort.

ents do grant bargain sell alien enfeoff and confirm unto the said David Ross one certain tract or parcel of land containing one thousand acres, be the same more or less in the county of Fayette, on the branch of the Ohio River called the big bone creek including the large buffaloe lick about four miles from the Ohio River. Beginning at a large red oak and white hickory, near the creek thence south five degrees west four hundred and eighty poles to a sugar tree and hickory saplin thence south forty seven degrees west, one hundred and eighty poles crossing a branch to a red oak near the mud lick, north seventy five degrees west one hundred and sixty poles crossing the great bone creek to a lynn on the hill side north four hundred and ninety nine poles to a sugar tree and black ash, north eighty degrees east three hundred and thirty poles to the beginning, with its appurtenances.

To have and to hold the said tract of land with all and singular the premises with the appurtenances unto the said David Ross his heirs and assigns forever, and the aforesaid bargained land unto the said David Ross his heirs and assigns forever, they the said William Christian and Anna, his wife, shall and will warrant and forever defend, free from the claim and demand of all persons whatever. In witness where of, the said parties have set their hands and seals the day above mentioned.

                              William Christian   (LS)
                              Anna Christian   (LS)

Signed, sealed & delivered
before
        William Dandridge
        J. Mosby
        John Harvie
        Isham Williams

With the sale and transfer of title to 1000 acres including Big Bone Lick for so considerable a sum as $4455.00 in 1780, there naturally arises the question as to what value did the pioneers attach to the Big Bone salt springs in the wilderness of *Kentucke*. Did Christian in fact profit well by this transaction? To put the query is to require an answer in some amount of coin of the realm, or goods in trade, since it was largely for speculation that the early adventurers of Virginia risked their lives in the primeval forests of the Ohio Valley. Fortunately, the early records of Jefferson County reveal a similar transaction. This was the sale and transfer from Robert Daniel to Richard Jones Waters in 1785 of 1000 acres "near Big Bone, at the rate of twenty-five pounds per 100 acres of Virginia currency."

Here, it will be readily seen, is the key to contemporary appraisal of Big Bone itself. Colonel Christian's 1000 acres survey of 1774, excluding Big Bone Lick, because Daniel's land, though probably first class Ohio River bottoms, possessed no such attraction, was worth about £250 in terms of the Daniel-Waters deal. This rendered into the new dollar currency of the infant United States at the then customary rate of exchange of $3.30 to the Virginia pound sterling, sets a value of about eighty-three and a quarter cents per acre on Colonel Christian's land at Big Bone. But he sold it at about $4.45½ cents per acre—a net increase of $3.62 per acre solely because of the saline springs. Or, taking the transaction as a whole, the difference between the selling price of these two adjacent 1000 acre tracts, one sold by Christian for £1350 and the other by Daniel for £250 was £1100 in favor of the Big Bone lands. This is equivalent

BIG BONE LICK

to saying that these famous springs for their salt content alone—not their fossils—were worth, prior to the year 1800, $3,630.00.

But in these troublesome times one hundred and fifty years ago with the outcome of American Revolution still undetermined, hard money, particularly in far away *Kentucke,* was always a difficult, sometimes an impossible, thing to get. So, frequently, land deals, while fixing a consideration in currency, also set up an alternative in trade of goods. This was provided in the transfer from Daniel to Waters, as their old contract[5] shows. It may also have been the case at the time of the transfer of other lands in the vicinity of Big Bone Lick; but of this we now have no absolute proof.

Agreement between Robert Daniel and Richard Jones Waters, both of Jefferson Co. Daniel is to sell to Waters 1000 acres of land, part of a 5000 or 6000 acre survey which Daniel has right and title to on Ohio River near the Big Bone, at rate of £25 per 100 acres Virginia currency, to be surveyed in two tracts of 500 acres each, not to adjoin each other, and deed to be made out with a clause of warranty against claims "from the beginning of the world up to time of conveyance." For this Waters obligates himself to pay certain money or the following articles; flour at 30 shillings per 100; whiskey at 6 shillings per gallon; shrub at 10 shillings per quart; castings at 1 shilling 3 pence per lb.; bar-iron at 1 shilling 3 pence per lb. The money is to be paid by the fall boating in 1786 and 1787; if not in money, then in aforesaid articles. Feb. 14, 1785. WITNESSES: Benjamin Earickson, Stephen Smith, Recorded April Court, 1785.

---
[5] *Calendar of Bond and Power of Attorney, Book I, Jefferson County, Kentucky, 1783-1798.* P. 26, Ludie J. Kinkead and Katherine G. Healy, Filson Club Quarterly, Vol. VII, pp. 41-42. Louisville.

Speculation in wild lands in Kentucky evidently did not always turn out satisfactorily for David Ross, who, it may be remarked, was a large operator, his possession west of the Alleghenies totalling on two occasions, at least, as evidenced by sales, considerably in excess of 100,000 acres. On the thirtieth of July, 1806, he deeded all of his "estate in the County of Bourbon in the State of Kentucky called and well known by the name of Bigg Bone Lick, containing about two thousand acres on the bigg bone creek and four thousand acres on the Ohio, the whole located and surveyed under old military Warrants" to Wilson Allen, Edmund W. Rootes, and Jacob Myers in discharge of an old debt of fourteen thousand dollars and interest. This old land instrument,[6] a quaint piece of writing, may be seen in one of the oldest record books of the Clerk's office of the Kentucky Court of Appeals at Frankfort. While in effect a deed, it did not, in fact, immediately convey physical possession of Big Bone Lick and the lands surrounding, this being reserved to David Ross until August 1, 1808. Since interest was specified to be paid with principal on this date, by means of a public sale if necessary, it was in effect a mortgage. As such it left Ross in possession of the "Big Bones" and made it possible for him to accede to the exploratory request of President Jefferson in February, 1807.

[6] *Old Kentucky Entries and Deeds.* Willard Rouse Jillson, Filson Club Pubs. No. 34, p. 526, Louisville, 1926; and Deed Book L, pp. 12, 13, 14, 15, and 16, office of Clerk of the Court of Appeals of Kentucky, Frankfort.

SALT MAKING AND SOCIAL
ACTIVITIES

VII

Salt Making and Social Activities

"Idlers who come to loiter, drink, bathe, and kill the game."

About the time that Kentucky attained Statehood, 1792, the population of that portion of the Ohio Valley touching upon Kentucky had grown so enormously that all of the heavy manufactured commodities required by a pioneering people such as salt, lead, and iron came to have a very high value. Salt particularly because of its perishable nature was freighted over the Alleghenies only with great difficulty and at an excessive cost. Consequently the demand for the homemade variety, as foreseen a decade earlier by Colonel Christian, strengthened until considerable industries were built up around the more accessible salt springs of the Commonwealth.

This was particularly true at Bullitt's Lick on the Salt River, Drennon's Lick on the Kentucky River, Blue Licks on the Licking, and at Big Bone. Here close to the Ohio River where the aborigines had gathered from time immemorial, where Mary Inglis had taken part in a Shawnee salt boiling in 1756, where Daniel Boone, Simon Kenton, George Rogers Clark, and others had played their part in many a forced march and salt making, a new day dawned for an age-old human industry. Although the natural brines in this locality were never really very saline—it took about five or six hundred gallons to produce one bushel of salt[1]—the low price of labor, the cheapness of fuel, and the central location of these salt springs at Big Bone operated in their favor during the

---

[1] *History of Kentucky.* Richard Collins, Vol. II, p. 52. Covington, 1882.

period of settlement. And further, their close proximity to the Ohio River and the newly established town opposite the mouth of the Licking, which General Arthur St. Clair had made his military headquarters and renamed Cincinnati, gave them decided commercial advantage.

Consequently one is not much surprised to see the saline springs at Big Bone, which, during the glacial age and later, had drawn the great hoofed beasts hundreds of miles across the central interior of this continent, and in the pre-historic and historical periods had proven a mecca for countless bands of roving copper-hued savages and pale-faced hunters and explorers, become the center of a well established salt industry in the support of the rapidly growing and expanding civilization of the west. Replacing the Indian's earthen chard and the small iron boiling kettles of the first pioneers, flat, evaporating furnaces, designed to more rapidly concentrate the brines and precipitate the salt, were constructed close to the original springs.

About this time Big Bone took on a new and earnest aspect of activity. Wood cutters working in the surrounding forests supplied the fuel; furnace tenders kept up the fires, replenished the brines and shoveled out into bushel baskets the gathering salt. Mule teams with diamond-hitched back packs then took up the burden and, travelling a perfectly wretched road, transported the product to the mouth of the Licking. Here the salt from Big Bone was transferred to boats of various kinds plying the waters of the Ohio. A review of the files of some of the first Ohio Valley newspapers reveals that, as early as April 15, 1794, "good old Kentucky salt" was advertised for sale in Cincinnati.[2] Thus again, as in the more remote past,

[2] *History of Kentucky.* Richard Collins, Vol. I, p. 24, Covington, 1882.

BIG BONE LICK 89

and from the earliest times, did Big Bone become well and widely known. Operated in a desultory way for its salt, which commanded a good price in the new settlements of the country, it was manned and frequented by a rough and ready group of fellows who spent their work-a-day life in laborious dirt and sweat, and their oft-recurring periods of leisure in cursing and fighting and drunken brawls.

During the passage of nearly a century and a half much of the detail pertaining to the early land transactions and salt-making operations at Big Bone Lick has been irretrievably lost. Yet some definite facts and a few traditions persist. From these an outline, at least, of times and affairs in this part of northern Kentucky can be reconstructed. It appears that by some means James Douglas, who, it will be recalled, Hanson asserted, had made the Big Bone survey in 1774 for Colonel William Christian, had come into possession of land at the famous lick. The oldest Jefferson County entry books show he entered upon 500 acres[3] there May 22, 1780. Then in 1793 came Douglas' death at the hands of Indians and the land and the lick passed to his daughter. Perhaps at this juncture it might be well to let old "Eph" Sandusky,[4] one of Kentucky's early pioneers, tell something of the story of Douglas' surveying and exploring party in 1774, and the first salt making at Big Bone, as he did many years ago to one of Kentucky's great historians, the Reverend John D. Shane:[5]

[3] *Old Kentucky Entries and Deeds.* Willard Rouse Jillson, p. 200, Filson Club Pubs. No. 34. Louisville, 1926.

[4] Originally and interchangeably in early days spelled *Sowdusky* and *Sodowsky.*

[5] *John D. Shane's Interview with Ephraim Sandusky.* Lucien Rule (Draper MSS., Kentucky Papers, 11CC 141-45. Madison, Wis.). Filson Club Quart., pp. 220-222, Vol. VIII, Louisville, 1934.

James Douglas, the surveyor, was killed. His heir was an only daughter. All the estate fell into David Ross' hands. Thomas Carneal was Ross' agent. Douglas' daughter lost her virtue and married a worthless man who thought only of her fortune, and David Ross easily found means of gettin' it from him. Douglas had this survey at the Big Bone [Big Bone Lick, Boone County]. My father [Jacob Sandusky] never got a cent till the agents came to get him to show them their corner. My father said the estate owed him £40, and he never would go unless they would give him half his wages and also an overcoat for one which had been burned at a sugar camp when they were making sugar. [Old] Tom, father of Tom Carneal was one of the salt makers. Davis Carneal was partner with David Ross in Big Bone: My father went down and superintended the making of salt in 1797-8 and 9, three years. Carneal, however, had started the furnaces and put up kettles before that time.

Douglas' surveying party: [consisted of] 1. John Smith, [who] was the last of the party that died. 2. Isaac Hite. 3. Willis, from Virginia. 4. Mordicia Batson, or Matson, 5. .... 6. .... 7. and Jacob Sandusky.

Jacob Sandusky and party went down the river in two canoes [in 1774]. When they got to the Falls [of the Ohio] they sent forward my father and John Smith to see if there were any signs of Indians that would prevent their making a portage. They came to a little path; the night previous it had rained, and there they saw the fresh tracks where the Indians had come down that morning for water. They knew the Indians' incampment must be somewhere near in the bottom there. They first pushed off their canoes, got in, and went on down over the Falls, thinking if death was to be, it would be preferable being drowned to be massacred.

While they were on the bank of the Mississippi [later] at Orleans they overheard two men, captains, who were pass-

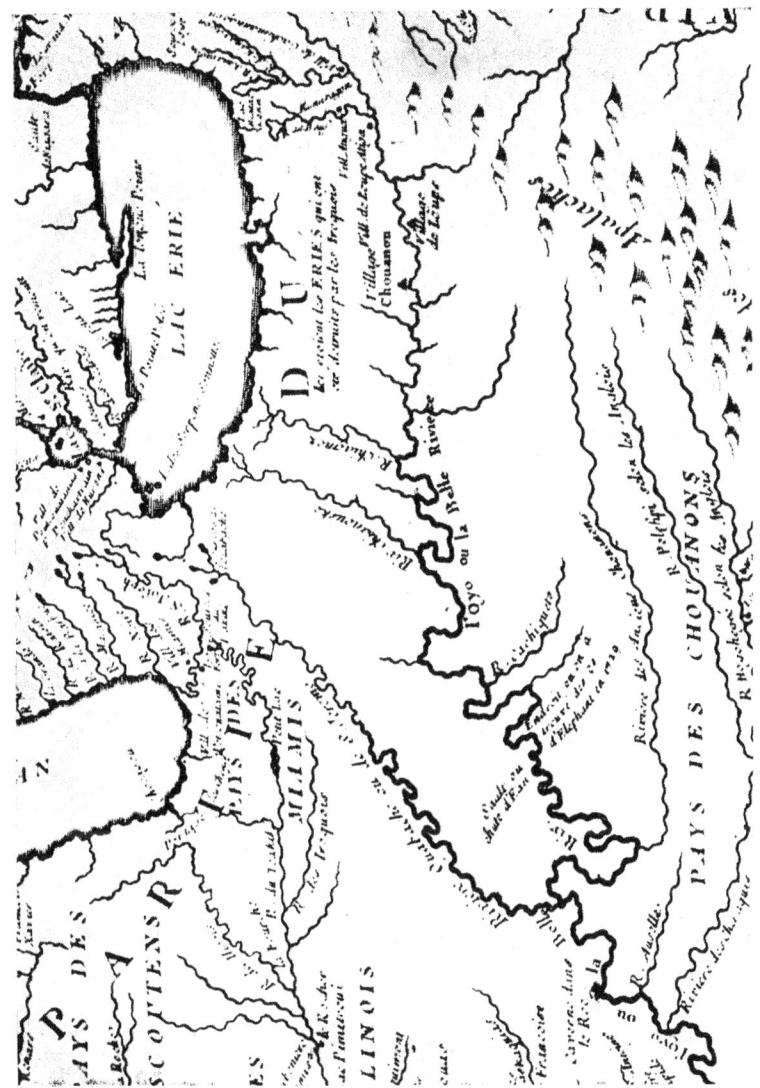

A PORTION OF J. N. BELLIN'S MAP OF 1744

Entitled *Carte de la Louisiane Cours doMississipi et Pais Voisins*
This facsimile reproduction, it will be noted, carries the following statement "Endroit ou on à trouvé des os d'Elephant en 1729" (The place where they found the elephant's bones in 1729). The citation was taken by Bellin from the Ohio River notes of M. Chaussegros de Lery who was the first to record M. de Longueil's discovery of Big Bone Lick. Bellin made a slight geographical error in locating the "Place." It should have been a little northeast of "R." in R. Cachiquete which he seems to have intended to represent the Kentucky River.

ing along, in conversation. One remarked they looked like people in distress. The other replied there were hundreds of such people along the Mississippi. Well, they were God's people, said the first captain, and he would see who they were. He obtained from them a narrative of their adventure, took them on his vessel and carried them around to New York. On their way, when they had gotten far towards New York they one day discovered an elephant's tooth. My father replied that he had seen just such things at Big Bone. When the Captain heard this he took him into his room and obtained a full statement of the whole affair relating to Big Bone. On their final parting the Captain opened his chest of money and told them just to take whatever they would need. I don't know whether he ever got anything back.

After twenty-six years of ownership and operation of Big Bone Lick, with what was probably indifferent success due to the pioneering nature of the country and the lack of good travelable roads to the interior of Kentucky, David Ross sold this famous spring and two thousand acres of land to three gentlemen in Tidewater, Virginia.[6] The transaction took place July 30, 1806. It was about this time that President Jefferson was beginning to interest himself, through Dr. Wistar of Philadelphia and Dr. Goforth of Cincinnati, in the paleontology of this famous lick. An interesting description of Big Bone Lick as it appeared early in the nineteenth century is here reproduced from an early issue of the *Navigator:*[7]

BIG BONE LICK

There are places at Big Bone Lick, where the salt water bubbles up through the earth, that are rendered a

[6] *Old Kentucky Entries and Deeds.* Willard Rouse Jillson, Filson Club Pubs. No. 34, p. 526. Louisville, 1926.
[7] *The Navigator.* Zadok Cramer, p. 202. Pittsburgh, 1811.

perfect quagmire admitting nothing heavier walking over them than geese or other light web-footed fowl. Cattle dare not venture nearer than to their edges. One of these places appears bottomless for no soundings have ever been found. Throw in a 10 ft. rail endwise, and it buries itself; another embraces near a quarter of an acre, over which grows a very fine and short grass. May it not be reasonable to account for so many of the mammoths bones being deposited at this place, by presuming that in their seeking the salt water, and venturing a little too far, or otherwise that their own enormous weight pushing them forward too far for recovery, and sinking, thus were buried one after another, to the number we now find their remnants. The places where their bones are now found are tolerably hard from filling up by the washings of the small stream which runs through them, and from having been much dug up and the mud exposed to the sun.

Mr. Colquohoun, a Scotch gentleman, resides at, and owns, this singular spot of ground; and has two extensive salt furnaces at work, which are able to make about 60 bushels per day, notwithstanding the weakness of the water. Mr. Colquohoun has been at much labor and expense in fixing his furnaces in a superior stile, particularly in the retention of heat, and saving the fuel. His kettles are of an oblong square, coming to about half the size at bottom that they are at the top; they hold about 12 or 15 gals., and are fixed close together in a double row, having their edges covered with sheet lead lapped down closely on all sides, so as to prevent any heat from escaping; the fuel is introduced into a grated furnace, whose mouth is closed by an iron door.—The kettles rise gradually from the front to the chimney, so as to occasion a sufficient draught of air. The first kettle in the furnace is round and contains about 100 gallons, and as this receives the greatest degree of heat, and evaporates the water much faster than the smaller ones, they are partly supplied from it after the water has boiled down considerable, and the small black kettles are supplied from those near the front. The kettles are filled with salt water in the first instance from a wooden pipe running over the middle of the furnace, having a spigot hole on each side; this is supplied by a pipe, from the general reservoir filled from the leading troughs. Mr. Colquohoun was engaged in September 1810, in boring for salt water and had got 150 feet through solid rock with an inch and a half auger.

The Big Bone Lick is in the state of Kentucky, 20 miles from Cincinnati on the road leading from that town to the falls of Ohio. The land about it is flat and cold, with scrubby timber, and there is no cleared ground in view of the Lick, not even a garden; notwithstanding, it is worth a visit to the curious, and the superior intelligence and hospitality of its worthy proprietor makes such a visit well paid for. The back water, in the very high stages of the Ohio, has been known to inundate this place, and extend for some distance above it.

With the gradual settling of the Middle West the salt industry at Big Bone Lick began to languish. This was due to a number of causes, chief of which was the weakness of the natural brines. It has been stated[8] that it required five or six hundred gallons of salt water from Big Bone springs or wells to make a single bushel of salt. Early in the nineteenth century rich salt deposits were discovered elsewhere in the Ohio Valley and at points, as in West Virginia, where the cost of production was less and the volume of recovery was greater. These new operations closed the door on salt manufactories at Big Bone Lick and the business was finally abandoned in this locality about 1812. For a while interest in Big Bone

---
[8] *History of Kentucky.* Lewis Collins, p. 181. Maysville and Cincinnati, 1850.

apparently lapsed. Rafinesque found the place rather dull, the old inn and the springs being patronized only by nondescript sportsmen, when he visited it in 1821.[9] He wrote:

> The water at the Lick Springs contains salt and sulphur; it has a bluish cast—an abominable taste, although readily drunk by the idlers who come—to loiter, drink, bathe, and kill the game—very plenty yet on the hills.

Upwards of a hundred years ago Big Bone Lick was one of the most celebrated health and watering resorts in this part of the Ohio Valley. Coupled with its sulphur-saline spring water, which demonstratedly possesses mild medicinal properties, the historic background of the salt-making period and the prehistoric association afforded by the more or less continuous recovery of the bones of the mammoth and the mastodon, served to draw to this secluded spot in Boone County representatives of the best families in Kentucky, and adjacent parts of Ohio and Indiana. Into the beautiful valley of Big Bone Creek, which the earliest pioneers had described as encompassing some of the richest land of the Bluegrass, came the family coaches of the Breckinridges,[10] Todds, Crittendens, Clays, Marshalls, McDowells, and many others from over the Commonwealth of Kentucky in those glamorous antebellum days now so far away.

These sparkling equipages carrying the beauty and chivalry of their day, piled high with luggage and driven by old slaves in linen or livery, rolled along a dusty ridge road.

---

[9] *Visit to Big-Bone Lick, in 1821.* C. S. Rafinesque. Month. Am. Jour. of Geol., Vol. 1, pp. 355-358. July, 1831.

[10] *Big Bone Lick Once Gathering Place of Chivalry of the South.* George F. Beard, Ed. Kentucky Weekly. Louisville, Kentucky, January 4, 1935.

BIG BONE LICK

This thoroughfare, following a generally north and south course, later became known as the Lexington-Covington toll pike. It is now the Dixie Highway. Between the villages of Florence and Walton these vacation-bound vehicles bore to the west and soon were threading their way through the narrow streets of the quaint old town of Union. Continuing on to the west and southwest over a rolling grassy plateau they turned suddenly to the south and came down a winding forested hill directly into the sequestered hamlet of Big Bone. While many, perhaps the most, of the summer visitors to these springs, during the middle of the last century, came by this upland route, a good many others followed the meandering course of the Ohio River. This was particularly true of those coming from Ohio and Indiana. Gay parties arrived not infrequently in private barges; but the bulk of the river travellers came on the steamboats of those days. River captains then made regular stops at Hamilton Landing on the Ohio River. This place is about a mile and a half west of the licks.

River travellers, clambering up the banks at Hamilton, then followed a narrow country road either afoot or by hack over a low divide and came at last to stop, perhaps for a week or two, at the Clay House. This rambling old structure standing west of the springs and the old road to Louisville at Big Bone had been built shortly after 1800 and was named in honor of Henry Clay, the great statesman of Lexington, Kentucky. Here, at Big Bone, in those old days before intersectional strife arose to rend the unity and common peaceful purpose of the country, life—particularly during the fashionable summer season—went along in a smooth stream of unaffected pleasure and good living. Northeast of the hotel with its spacious veranda overlooking the valley and the lick, and across the road, a row of bath houses stood on a bit of level ground bordering the main creek and the marsh or "jelly ground" that surrounded the famous old salt springs.

In those days, now gone and all but forgotten, the ground about the lick was covered with smooth-growing green turf, while the lick itself, brown in the summer sun, covered an irregular area of several acres. In a delightful grove of oaks and elms spreading their cooling shade over a low mound between the spring and the main village street of Big Bone, there stood at that time a large open frame pavilion. Here in the cool after-supper hours of the evening to the accompaniment of Negro fiddling and the clapping of many hands, was frequently danced the minuet, the lancers, and the changeful Virginia reel.

But the popularity of the place rapidly waned and not quite a score of years later—in 1847—the place was deserted. Judge Lewis Collins, writing during the mid-century, said in an artless and somewhat melancholy vein:[11] "The springs at this place have been considerably frequented on account of their medicinal virtues; but at this time no accommodation of any sort for visitors is kept there, and but very inadequate accommodation is to be found anywhere in the neighborhood." What a picture of abandonment! Though nearly a century has slipped away since they were penned, there is in these lines much which, in truth, is still applicable to Big Bone Lick.

[11] *Historical Sketches of Kentucky.* Lewis Collins, p. 181. Maysville and Covington, 1847-1850.

Today beneath the widespreading branches of this leafy grove on bright moonlight nights in mid-summer, one can still catch the spirit of those far-away proud days. Though the original hotel that stood there in 1830 is gone entirely, and another of more recent construction on the hill above the road north of the springs has long been disused and is rapidly falling into decay, an unusual charm still distinguishes this quaint old place. In the silver-flecked shadows of an occasional rustic bower or darkened trysting place, now overgrown with honeysuckle or wild roses, one unconsciously re-creates, as it were, the erstwhile moving scene of youthful amours and lighthearted gaiety. Under the spell of these old associations and a resurgence of the atmosphere of Kentucky's golden days, imaginative figures, gallant and colorful in silk, satin, and broadcloth, return to tread again, in these once happy haunts at Big Bone, the measured cadences of the dance. During such rare and happy moments, memory moving fancy free sweeps away, as if by some swift magic, all the garishness and dilapidation of the present scene and calls back from the vanished years, like an unforgetable fragrance, those bright assemblies of the past, pulsing deeply with the love, adventure, and romance of the old aristocratic South.

GEOLOGY AND PALEONTOLOGY

VIII

Geology and Paleontology

"The oldest believable Indian tradition failed."

Each of the great fossil localities of the world, at one time or another, has excited the active interest of man. To discover such places he has made long journeys to remote territories and suffered much in the way of personal hardship. His apparently natural inclination in this direction has usually identified itself firstly with viewing and collecting the relic bones of the ancient or extinct animals. Critical determination of genera and species based upon osteological comparison has then invariably followed. Close upon this has come detailed description and a careful figuring of all new types. To these basic studies he has added thoughtful speculations as to life habit, ancestral stocks, and migratory movements of the old beasts, and these interpretations have given to this type of writing peculiar charm. Such studies, when taken in their entirety, are spoken of as paleontology. To most intelligent human beings it is one of the most fascinating and romantic fields of scientific investigation, whether pursued professionally or in a purely avocational way.

Within recent years it has become customary to examine and describe the surrounding rocks, gravels, muds, and the associated physical and topographical features of any new fossil locality simultaneously with the work of collecting and classifying the bones. But formerly such was not the case. Within the memory of many men now living the discovery of a new and important fossil deposit was the signal for a mad scramble on the part of individual collectors, university and museum groups, to gather up as big a bag of bones as possible. Little or no thought at the time of collecting was turned toward the geology of the area producing the bone deposit. In many instances, as a matter of fact, this important correlated science was given no attention until years, perhaps generations, afterwards. Such was the case at Big Bone Lick.

Discovered in 1729 by a sturdy Frenchman commanding the provincial American troops of Louis XIII in a remote territory lying between New France and Louisiana, the gigantic fossils of this Ohio Valley locality soon became the subject of many a heated scientific controversy. These technical disputes flared up and died away while a whole century rolled on before any serious thought was given to the geology of the region. During this long lapse of time armed bands of savages and frontier militia crossed and recrossed this lick over the age-old buffalo trail which led from the Falls of the Ohio to the mouth of the Licking. General George Rogers Clark and numerous other early commanders of leather stockinged troops met and provisioned themselves here. Battles in the forest and bloody ambuscades came to mark this territory, and a rude earth fort was actually built by the pioneers on the island surrounded and protected by the moated waters of the creek and the quaking bog of the lick. Time passed and in the course of these military movements Big Bone actually passed under the possession of three flags, French, British, and American before the first geological observations of any moment were made in this vicinity.

At last at the end of the first quarter of the nineteenth century—in 1828—Professor William Cooper of New York

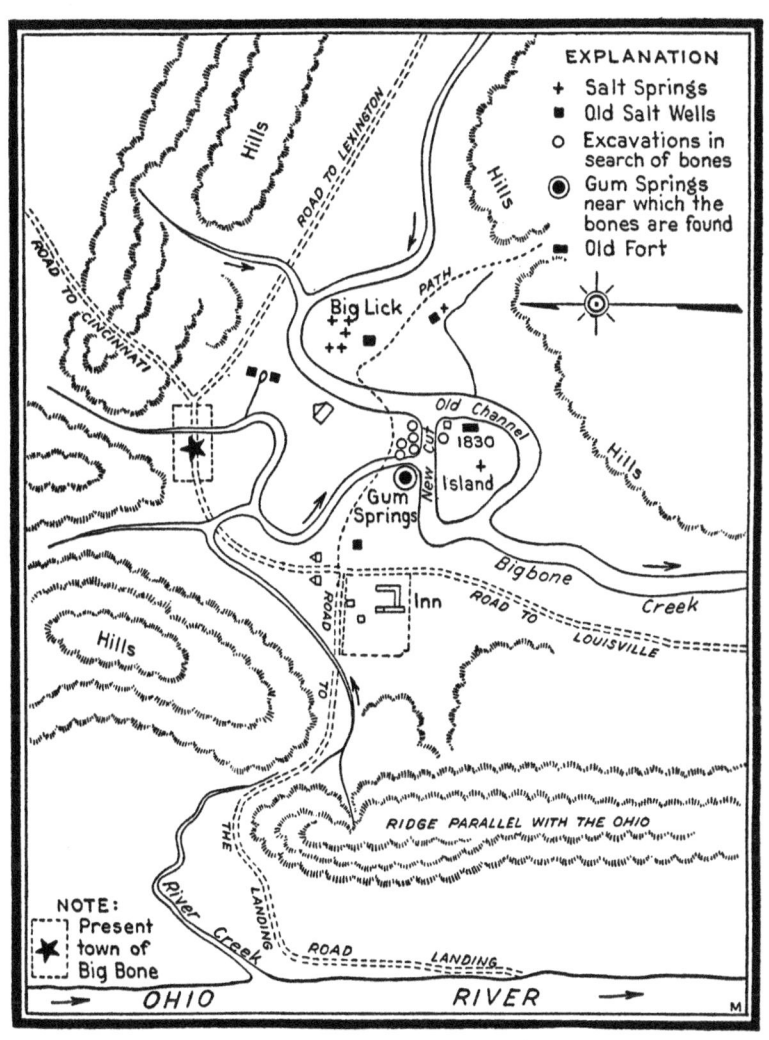

BIG BONE LICK AND ENVIRONS IN 1831
(Reproduced from William Cooper's Map)

BIG BONE LICK 105

City came to Big Bone Lick with eyes to see the geology of the area as well as the bones imbedded in the salty mud. In the course of a rather lengthy scientific article, issued in 1831, he wrote:[1]

> The substratum of the neighboring county is a limestone, abounding in organic remains. This appears at the surface on the sides and top of the hill, and along the banks of the great rivers..... At this lick, the valley is filled up to the depth of not less, generally, than thirty feet, with unconsolidated beds of earth of various kinds.

The uppermost of these alluvial beds he found to be a light yellow clay containing the bones of buffaloes and other recent animals. At greater depths in a darker colored, softer, and more gravelly layer, exhibiting the stems of reedy plants and the shells of fresh water mollusca, he found the bones of the extinct glacial animals.

Some fourteen years later, the noted English geologist, Charles Lyell, describing his *Travels in North America in the Years 1841-42*,[2] said:

> Two days after I reached Cincinnati, I set out, in company with two naturalists of that city, Mr. Buchanan and Mr. J. G. Anthony, who kindly offered to be my guides, in an excursion to a place of great geological celebrity in the neighboring State of Kentucky, called Big Bone Lick, where the bones of mastodons and many other extinct quadrupeds had been dug up in extraordinary aboundance.* * *

---

[1] *Notices of Big Bone Lick*. By William Cooper, Monthly Am. Jour. of Geology and Natural Science, Vol. I, No. 4, pp. 158-174, and No. 5, pp. 205-217. Philadelphia, 1831.

[2] *Travels in North America in the Years 1841-1842*. Charles Lyell, Vol. II, pp. 53-58. Wiley and Putnam, New York, 1845.

The lick is distant from Cincinnati about twenty-three miles in a South West direction. The intervening country is composed of the blue argillaceous limestone and marl before mentioned, the beds of which are nearly horizontal, and form flat table-lands intersected by valleys of moderate depth. In one of these, watered by the Big Bone Creek, occur the boggy grounds and springs called Licks. The term Lick is applied throughout North America to those marshy swamps where saline springs break out, and which are frequented by deer, buffalo, and other wild animals for the sake of the salt, whether dissolved in the water, or thrown down by evaporation in the summer season, so as to encrust the surface of the marsh. Cattle and wild beasts devour this incrustation greedily, and burrow into the clay impregnated with salt, in order to lick the mud.

The celebrated bog of Kentucky is situated in a nearly level plain, in a valley bounded by gentle slopes, which lead up to the table-lands before mentioned. The general course of the meandering stream which flows through the plain is from east to west. There are two springs on the southern or left bank, rising from marshes, and two on the opposite bank, the most western of which, called the Gum Lick, is at the point where a small tributary joins the principal stream. The quaking bogs on this side are now more than fifteen acres in extent, but all the marshes were formerly larger before the surrounding forest was partially cleared away. The removal of tall trees allowed the sun's rays to penetrate freely to the soil, and dry up part of the morass.

Within the memory of persons now living, the wild bisons or buffaloes crowded to these springs, but they have retreated for many years, and are now as unknown to the inhabitants as the mastodon itself. Mr. Phinnel,* the proprietor of the land, called our attention to two buffalo paths

---

*Spelled usually *Finnell*.

or trails still extant in the woods here, both leading directly to the springs. One of these in particular, which first strikes off in a northerly direction from the Gum Lick, is afterwards traced eastward through the forest for several miles. It was three or four yards wide, only partially overgrown with grass, and, sixty years ago, was as bare, hard, and well trodden as a high road.

The bog in the spots where the salt springs rise is so soft that a man may force a pole down into it many yards perpendicularly. It may readily be supposed, therefore, that horses, cows, and other quadrupeds, are now occasionally lost here; and that a much greater number of wild animals were mired formerly. In their eagerness to drink the saline waters and lick the salt, the heavy mastodons and elephants seem .... to have pressed upon each other, and sunk in these soft quagmires of Kentucky.

The greater proportion both of the entire skeletons of extinct animals, and the separate bones, have been taken up from black mud, about twelve feet below the level of the creek. It is supposed that the bones of mastodons found here could not have belonged to less than one hundred distinct individuals, those of the fossil elephant (*E. primigenius*), to twenty, besides which, a few bones of a stag, horse, megalonyx, and bison, are stated to have been obtained. Whether the common bison, the remains of which I saw in great numbers in a superficial stratum recently cut open in the river's bank, has ever been seen in such a situation as to prove it to have been contemporaneous with the extinct mastodon, I was unable to ascertain. In regard to the horse, it may probably have differed from our *Equus caballus* as much as the zebra or wild ass, in the same manner as that found at Newberne in North Carolina appears to have done. .... The greatest depth of the black mud has not been ascertained; it is composed chiefly of clay, with a mixture of calcareous matter and sand, and contains 5 parts in 100 of sulphate of lime, with some animal matter. (Cuvier, Oss. Foss., tom. i., p. 216.) Layers of gravel occur in the midst of it at various depths. In some places it rests upon the blue limestone. The only teeth which I myself procured from collectors on the spot, besides those of the buffalo, were recognized by Mr. Owen as belonging to extremely young mastodons. From the place where they were found, and the rolled state of some of the accompanying bones, I suspected that they had been washed out of the soil of the bogs above by the river, which often changes its course after floods.

Mr. Cooper of New York, who has given the fullest account of the fossils of this place, says, that the remains of reeds and freshwater mollusca accompany the bones; but he names no species of shells. Mr. Anthony and I were therefore diligent in our search for shells in pits which happened to have been recently laid open by collectors of fossil bones; and we soon obtained a small *Ancylus* and *Cyclas*. Afterwards, in the most eastern marsh, in the middle of which a powerful spring throws up beech nuts and shells from the mud below, we found two species of *Melania* known as Recent, *Physa heterostropha, Cyclas similis, C. dubia?* (and another species, not known to naturalists here), *Pisidium* (supposed to agree with one from Lake Erie), *Ancylus* (not known), and fragments of *Unio;* also the following land shells;—*Helix solitaria* (with bands of colour not effaced). *H. alternata, H. clausa, H. fraterna,* and *Pupa armifera.* As new terrestrial and freshwater shells are occasionally added to the recent American fauna, I think it very probable that all the fourteen species which we met with, and which, I believe, co-existed with the mastodon, are still living, though perhaps not all of them in the immediate neighborhood.

It is impossible to view this plain, without at once concluding that it has remained unchanged in all its principal features from the period when the extinct quadrupeds inhabited the banks of the Ohio and its tributaries. But one phenomenon perplexed us much, and for a time seemed quite unintelligible. On parts of the boggy grounds, a superficial covering of yellow loam was incumbent on the dark-coloured mud, containing the fossil bones. This partial covering of yellow sandy clay was at some points no less than fifteen or twenty feet thick. Mr. Bullock passed through it when he dug for fossil remains on the left bank of the creek, and he came down to the boggy grounds with bones below. We first resorted to the hypothesis that the valley might have been dammed up by a temporary barrier, and converted into a lake; but we afterwards learnt that, although the Ohio is seven miles distant by the windings of the creek, there being a slight descent the whole way, yet that great river has been known to rise so high as to flow up the valley of Big Bone Creek, and, so late as 1824, to enter the second story of a house built near the springs. The level of the Licks above the Ohio is about fifty feet, the distance in a straight line being only three miles. At Cincinnati the river has been known to rise sixty feet above its summer level, and in the course of ages it may occasionally have risen higher. It may be unnecessary, therefore, to refer to the general subsidence before alluded to (probably an event of a much older date), in order to account for the patches of superficial silt last described.

Several years after his geological and paleontological investigations in this area had been completed, Dr. N. S. Shaler, in reminiscent mood and with mature judgment wrote:[3]

About these springs there is generally a bit of swamp land, due to the slow down-sinking of the underlying rocks as they are deprived of a part of their solid matter by the

---
[3] *Kentucky; A Pioneer Commonwealth.* By N. S. Shaler, pp. 41-42, Boston and New York, 1884.

ascending springs. These swamps contain a wonderful collection of the bones of the large herbivora, which for ages resorted to these springs. Not only do we find the bones of the animals which occupied the country when the whites first came to it, the buffalo, the elk, the deer, etc.—but, also, deeper in the mire, or in positions that indicate a greater antiquity, great quantities of the bones of the fossil elephant, his lesser kinsman, the mastodon, the musk-ox, an extinct long-legged buffalo, the caribou, or American reindeer, and various other creatures which dwelt here in the time when the last glacial period covered the more northern region with a mantle of ice.

The largest, and to the geologist the most interesting, of these swamp-bordered springs is Big Bone Lick * * * situated in Boone County about twenty miles Southwest of Cincinnati, Ohio. At this point there is swampy low land around the salt springs that contains a wonderful mass of elephant, mastodon, bison, and other bones. Of the mammoth alone there are probably hundreds of skeletons, which were engulfed in the soft mud about the spring mouth, when, in the olden days, these great creatures resorted to this place for their annual salting. When the whites first came to the district the ground was thickly strewn with skeletons. The early settlers used them for supporting their camp kettles and for seats by the fireside.

Thus by easy stages of advancement we come down to modern times and present-day conceptions of the geology at Big Bone. To those of scientific bent who, in fair weather, enjoy a journey afield by foot, saddled steed, or motor car, the gentle hills and winding valleys of southwestern Boone County give friendly welcome. Approaching the area from the north over Kentucky State Highway Forty-two either through the hamlet of Union or Beaver Lick, one notices a

BIG BONE LICK   111

continuation of the blue even bedded fossiliferous limestones and shales found in the hills about Cincinnati and south of Newport and Covington. This is the Maysville formation, one of the upper stratigraphic divisions of the Ordovician rocks. Scattered over these hard sediments is a mantle of varying thickness of clay, sand, gravel, and boulder till. This is all glacial material brought to this country from Canada and the north by the continental ice sheet during the Pleistocene period. Between it and the underlying hard bedded limestones and shales of Maysville age a very extended series of sediments representing most of the Paleozoic, all of the Messozoic, and all of the Cenozoic are missing. The stratigraphic break thus recorded is the equivalent of many, many millions of years of earth history and proves beyond peradventure of doubt that, when the great ice cap nosed its way into northern Kentucky, this area had been a land area subject to the slowly beveling hand of erosion for a very long time.

As one comes down from the flat and frequently swampy upland levels into the inner and lower valleys of Big Bone Creek and its tributaries, he passes over rather thick beds of blue calcareous shales. These even bedded rocks with their thin slabby intercalated limestones are known as the Eden group. They are somewhat fossiliferous and easily eroded. They give rise to steep slopes and much washing and gullying with the result that poor straggling farms mark the Eden exposure not only in this region but elsewhere in Kentucky and adjacent parts of Ohio and Indiana. As shown in outcrop in this area the thickness of the Eden ranges from about 175 to nearly 200 feet.

In the bottoms of Big Bone Creek, alluviums of Recent and Pleistocene deposition are found in thicknesses varying from a few to upwards of a hundred feet or more as one approaches the shore line of the Ohio River. These loose sediments consist of sands, gravels, clays, and muds. They include the saline marls, oozes, and slimes of the salt licks and in thoroughly impregnated areas surrounding the springs give rise to the quaking bogs or "jelly ground" noted by all travellers to this district. It is in these loose and unconsolidated sediments covering to considerable depth the floor of the valley of Big Bone Creek in the vicinity of the salt springs that the bones of the great Pleistocene mammals have been found.

Beneath all the loose sediments and bedded rocks thus outlined, and quite unexposed at any point on the waters of Big Bone Lick Creek, lower Paleozoic beds of continuing Ordovician and, at greater depth, of Cambrian age extend downward at least several thousand feet. No igneous or metamorphic rocks are known in this region, except those occurring as boulders and pebbles in the mantle of glacial debris which sweeps broadly over this part of Kentucky. The saline water of the springs at Big Bone is therefore not in any way associated with intrusive rocks, but is simply the outpouring of age-old marine waters of deposition entombed in the lower Paleozoic sediments of this region, particularly in that significant Ordovician bed known as the Saint Peter sandstone. Its occurrence as a brine-saturated measure overriding at depths of about 800 to 1000 feet the axis of the Cincinnati arch a few miles to the east is the primary cause of the salt springs at Big Bone. But a contributing factor aiding in the accumulation of deep brines at Big Bone, and one of no mean importance, is the synclinal nature of the local geological structure[4]

---
[4] Structural Geologic Map of Boone County, Kentucky. Spencer Withers. Frankfort, 1931.

of this area. This, as well as the areal geology of the Big Bone area, may be seen depicted on two maps[5] recently issued by the Kentucky Geological Survey. Another and larger map[6] shows the extent of glaciation in this part of the Ohio Valley, and other interesting geological features.

Throughout North Central Kentucky—the Bluegrass Region—where they are most common, sulphur-saline waters, similar to or identical with those which have been flowing from the springs at Big Bone for countless ages, are generally known and spoken of as "Blue Lick." The name comes from the type locality at lower Blue Lick on the Licking River in Nicholas County, Kentucky. This celebrated locality, aside from its large fame in early Kentucky history, was formerly the site of one of the most notable watering places of the South. More recently the Blue Lick springs have ceased to flow with the result that interest in that particular locality as a spa has waned.

At Big Bone, however, while the volume of salt water, no doubt, is now somewhat diminished in its daily flow as compared to early times, it has been continuous. Here in the saline springs today, as in pre-historic times when great herds of hoofed wild beasts frequented them for their annual salting, this particular type of water carrying sulphur, salt, and lime in solution still rises under a natural hydrostatic head from the deep-seated Saint Peter. In its upward movement from its original source it passes slowly through a series of off-setting

---

[5] Geologic Map of Boone County, Kentucky. W. H. Shideler. Frankfort, 1931.

[6] Geologic Map of Kentucky. Willard Rouse Jillson, Scale 1:500,000. Frankfort, Kentucky, 1929.

joint planes and fissures of nearly vertical attitude which penetrate all of the superimposed bedded limestone rocks.

Because of the tendency of the many interbedded shales in this lower Ordovician series to seal the natural crevices in the massive limestones, occurrence of zones of fracture providing more or less continuous planes of egress for the saline-sulphur water imprisoned in the Saint Peter sandstone at depths of about 800 or 1000 feet below the surface are unusual in this part of the Ohio Valley except along major fault lines. Consequently saline springs of the type found at Big Bone are not common and springs so located as to emit their water under such a considerable cover of alluvium as is found in the lower waters of Big Bone Creek in close proximity to the Ohio are rare indeed. This combination of geological and geographic controls coupled with the important fact that the area of these licks, except for a relatively short period during one or two of the glacial advances, was not covered with a forbidding sheet of ice or deeply impounded water, set this area as a stage suitable to entice and trap the large mammals of the Pleistocene and more Recent times.

Some query has been raised as to how early in the glacial period the quaking bogs of Big Bone began to function as a place of entombment for North American animals. The question is not easily answered but it may be stated that, in all probability, none of the mammal remains exhumed in the vicinity of these licks antedate the Illinoian glacial stage. This does not mean that Pleistocene mammals were not present at Big Bone Lick during the earlier Nebraskan and Kansan epochs or their interglacial stages the Aftonian and the Yarmouth. It simply means that no representatives that are

BIG BONE LICK 115

ascribable without question to these early epochs have been found. Deeper excavations may later reveal them. Possibly, on the other hand, the main channel of the Ohio had not then been sufficiently trenched or flooded to back-fill with alluvium the area of the licks and thus provide a mirable thickness in the salty bogs.

If we take Cooper's account as a statement of fact, all of the bones of the early collectors came from a very limited area surrounding several prominent salt springs. They were found at the surface and down to depths of about twenty-five feet. Shaler working in the area nearly two score years later could find no order of bone deposition close to the springs, though he removed, as he said, and sent to the museum of Comparative Zoology at Harvard not less than a ton of fossils. At a point somewhat remote from the salt springs, now unmarked and forgotten, he did find, however, an order of deposition of creek mud and waste from the springs containing animal remains that apparently gave a suggestion as to the succession of the entombed animals. This was an important advance.

Certain fundamental limitations of knowledge, it must be borne in mind, operated to circumscribe Shaler's observations as to Big Bone Lick and its geology and paleontology. He apparently did not know, for instance, that the Illinoian advance of continental glaciation extended south of the Ohio River into Kentucky and over this area, for he so informed Professor Leidy[7] in the summer of 1870. Furthermore he held

[7] *Report on American Mastodon Remains in Warren Museum and Cambridge University Museum.* Joseph Leidy, September 6, 1870. Proc. Acad. Nat. Sc. Phila., p. 97. Philadelphia, 1870.

to the erroneous opinion that extensive beds of rock salt underlay the Big Bone region. The gradual solution of these saline deposits during the glacial epoch, he held, allowed the superimposed beds of limestone and shale to fall into a great cavity in which the animals were mired to their death.

It seems rather curious now that Shaler, a geologist of national reputation, could have been unaware of the extensive glacial deposits so prominently disposed in the valley of Woolper and Gunpowder Creeks just to the North of Big Bone, and so generally spread over the Bluegrass hills west of Beaver Lick on all sides of the celebrated salt licks down to the very waters of the Ohio River. Had he known this, the ponding of the waters of the Ohio over the licks for considerable and successive periods each year would have been plain to him and the rock salt-solution theory—a rather ingenious hypothecation—would have been unnecessary.

Although Big Bone Lick has come to enjoy a rather wide reputation, it has produced, it must be admitted, a relatively slender list of species of vertebrates, the number being about seventeen. The abundance of skeletal remains of *Mammut americanum, Elephas primigenius,* and *Elephas columbi* leave no doubt as to their presence at Big Bone. *Equus complicatus, Megalonyx jeffersoni, Bootherium bomifrons, Symbos cavifrons, Bison antiqus,* and *Bison bison,* are also quite as definitely identified. Cooper states that he saw traces of *Cervus canadensis, Odocoileus virginianus,* and *Alces americanus.* Recently the American peccary *Platygonus compressus* has been ascribed to Big Bone Lick, but the correctness of this the writer is inclined to doubt, since he has never seen a specimen from this locality. In this connection attention may be called to the fact that the following list contains no representatives of the canidae or felidae. It also lacks even a single species of the numerous family of rodents and of course exhibits no insectivores, aves, or reptilia. The entire list of the species of fossil mammals reported from Big Bone Lick as given by Hay[8] follows. The writer has appended to each the equivalent common name.

Edentata

Megalonyx jeffersonii, The giant Pleistocene ground sloth.
Mylodon harlani, The small glacial ground sloth.

Perissodactyla

Equus complicatus, The American Pleistocene horse.
Tapirus haysii, The Pleistocene tapir.

Artiodactyla

Odocoileus virginianus, The Virginia deer.
Cervus canadensis, The Roosevelt elk or wapiti.
Cervalces scotti, The "stag-moose" or reindeer.
Alces americanus, The moose.
Rangifer caribou, The caribou.
Bootherium bombifrons, The Pleistocene musk-ox.
Symbus cavifrons, The musk-ox.
Bison antiqus, The large glacial bison or buffalo.
Bison bison, The small modern bison or buffalo.

Proboscidia

Mammut americanum, The Pleistocene mastodon.
Elephas primigenius, The small Siberian mammoth.
Elephas columbi, The large American mammoth.

---

[8] *The Pleistocene of North America, etc.*, by O. P. Hay, Carnegie Institution of Washington, Pub. No. 322, p. 403. Washington, February, 1923.

Carnivora

Ursus americanus, The American black bear.

Important as a paleontological check list of the orders, suborders, genera, and species, such as that given above, may be for any well known fossil locality, the average reader will always find less in it to impress him than in some general feature of perhaps only incidental importance associated with the deposit. Thus it is at Big Bone. The occurrence here of upwards of a dozen and a half separate Pleistocene mammalian species really commands no attention at all compared with the interest manifested in the story of the romantic discovery of this lick or in the vivid early pen-pictures of its bone-strewn surface. Similarly numerous books and pamphlets describing with exactness and detail the comparative anatomy and osteology of its erstwhile giant denizens rot on their shelves unopened while other much less dependable pieces of writing re-creating the vanished aboriginal scene adorned with highly colored bits of imagination are well known and widely read.

Happily at Big Bone Lick, it has always been patent to even the most casual observer delving into the history of the locality that many, many bones, skulls, teeth, and tusks have been removed from this area. This has usually captured his interest which upon further investigation has been increased by descriptions of the rather occasional *Megalonyx*, the rare *Bootherium*, and the giant *Proboscidia*. Usually he has paid little attention to the very noteworthy, though less apparent, fact that in no instance has the complete skeleton of any single individual been recovered at Big Bone. Over a hundred years ago it was estimated after a careful check of the fossil bones that had been removed had been completed that they represented in the *Proboscidia* alone at least one hundred mastodons and twenty mammoths.

But today when we consider the several very early collections, such as that of Colonel Croghan, General Harrison, and others which were either entirely lost or partly destroyed, and add that inescapably large but unknown number of individuals whose skeletons must have been broken up and borne away during the ages by the flood waters of Big Bone Creek, conservative calculations surely double the figures given above and approximate the reasonable total of at least two hundred and fifty individuals of the two extinct tribes of elephants alone. Add to this the smaller beasts—those whose bones were not as large as the great Proboscidians and consequently less frequently preserved—the musk ox, the horse, the moose, the caribou, the elk, the giant sloth, the buffalo, and the deer, as well as the many that have not yet been recovered, and the number of animals that met disaster and death at Big Bone Lick must be conceded to run far beyond the hundreds and into the thousands of individuals.

Such a profusion of bones! Such a multiplicity of individuals! Such a charnal house in nature! Born of such reflections comes a very natural query as to the cause of the extinction of the great herds of mammoths and mastodons that ranged through the southern part of the Ohio Valley during the latter part of the glacial epoch and probably for some time thereafter. Any answer to this question must fail of absolute proof and will, therefore, be less positive than could be desired. It is, perhaps, sufficient to say that the rather considerable change of climate which followed the recession of the continental ice sheet—the coming in of increasingly warmer and dryer summers, of shorter and milder winters—and the advent of prehistoric man with his growing intelligence brought about the seemingly rapid decline of these ancient elephants. As the individuals fell the number and size of the herds decreased, thus affording less and less protection to the young, and hastening the day of ultimate extinction. Ponderous in movement and slow in reproduction, the break-down of the herd caused by a slowly changing and uncompromising environment to which they could not adjust themselves brought about finally their disappearance from the primeval paths of the great grassy plains and the far-flung broad-leafed forests.

Early man, roaming the North American wasteland—savage, lustful, and cruel—delighted, then as now, in the primitive sports of the chase and the kill. Obeying the urge of hunger or the wanton desire to destroy he followed relentlessly these slow-moving archaic remnants of the American Pleistocene that had survived the passing of the climate and environment to which nature through countless ages had adjusted them. Swarming in bands of pestiferous fighters, he attacked them, prodding them on with an endless barrage of clubs, stones, and in some instances with spears and arrows. Occasionally—possibly not infrequently—whole tribes drove these great tusked mammals for many miles until, weary of flight and plagued to distraction, they plunged over a cliff or into some deep morass to their sudden doom. Such may have been the case occasionally, during prehistoric times in the immediate vicinity of Big Bone Lick, though collectors, to date, have failed to recover any paleolithic artifacts among the big bones.

Primeval killings of this type regularly practiced in this quaking, slushy bog at Big Bone would, however, have measurably added to the natural assemblage of disconnected skeletal parts which have been found in this area during the relatively short period of its occupancy by civilized man. But the human hand need not have been an important contributing agent in the vast accumulation of bones in this famous Kentucky bog, for the salty water and the deep quagmire maintained by the intermittently flooded waters of the nearby Ohio were sufficient—the one as a bait, the other as a trap—to catch and hold the ponderous beasts of that far-away time. In the grand sweep of the unrecorded years following the retreat of the glacial ice sheet in this region, mammoth, mastodon, horse, sloth, and ox all passed away and with them every trace of primitive man. When the earliest white men came into this part of Kentucky, Ohio, and Indiana, the oldest believable Indian tradition failed utterly in its explanation of the enigmatic post-glacial tragedy of Big Bone Lick.

ANNOTATED BIBLIOGRAPHY OF
BIG BONE LICK

Annotated Bibliography
GEOLOGY, PALEONTOLOGY, AND HISTORY

ADAMS, LEITH
1. *The British Fossil Elephants:* Palaeontographical Soc., Vol. XXXIII, pp. 75, 122. London, May, 1879.
   References and comparisons of Big Bone Lick mammoth or mastodon molars in the British Museum and the Woodwardian Museum at Cambridge. Citations from Cuvier as to proboscidian teeth from Big Bone Lick. (U. S. G. S. Lib.)

ADLER, CYRUS
2. *Jefferson as a Man of Science:* Vol. XIX, pp. iii-x, in the *Writings of Thomas Jefferson.* Washington, 1904.
   Describes Jefferson's interest as a paleontologist in the fossils collected at Big Bone Lick.

ALLEN, J. A.
3. *The American Bison, Living and Extinct:* pp. v-ix, and 1-231, Memoirs, Kentucky Geological Survey, Vol. I, pt. 2, Cambridge, 1876; also Harvard Uni. Mus. Comp. Zoology, Vol. IV. Cambridge, Mass., 1876.
   A detailed, systematic monograph with 12 plates and map on the bisons with many references to those found at Big Bone Lick.

ALLEN, WILLIAM B.
4. *A History of Kentucky:* pp. 19, 113, 114. Louisville, 1872.
   Refers to salt water and fossil bones of the mammoth and mastodon, evidently rewritten from Collins, Marshall, and other earlier Kentucky historians.

AMERICAN PHILOSOPHICAL SOCIETY
5. *Proceedings of the American Philosophical Society (of) Philadelphia:* Vol. XXII, Part III, pp. 123 (Nicola), 193 (Matlock), 388 (Wiston, Jefferson), 390 (Goforth, Brown, Jefferson, Peale, and Vaughan), 394 (Jefferson, Wiston, Vaughan), 413 (Jefferson's coll. from Big Bone Lick), 414 (Wiston's papers on Big Bone Lick Fossils lost; advertised for by librarian). Philadelphia, 1885.
   Many references to Big Bone Lick and early collections therefrom. An important source. (U. S. G. S. Lib.)

ASHE, THOMAS
6. *Memoirs of Mammoth and various other extraordinary and stupendous bones, Incognita, or non-descript animals found in the vicinity of the Ohio, etc.:* 60 pp. Liverpool, 1806.

BIBLIOGRAPHY

A grandiloquent piece of writing, attempting to be scientific but actually a composite piracy of the writings of Collinson, Jefferson, Peale, Buffon, Hunter, Turner, and others on Big Bone Lick fossils (p. 40) which he, Ashe, stole from Dr. Goforth, of Cincinnati. (U. S. G. S. Lib.)

7. *Travels in America:* Pp. 209-210. London, 1808.
Reference to the quality of the water at Big Bone Lick.

BARTON, BENJAMIN SMITH

8. *Miscellaneous Facts and Observations:* The Philadelphia Med. and Phys. Jour., Vol. I, pp. 154-159. Philadelphia, 1805.
Describes fossil bones at Big Bone Lick. Quotes from the letter of John Bartram to James Logan. Shawnee Indians had brought a tooth and part of a tusk to Fort Pitts. They reported five whole skeletons at Big Bone and a shoulder blade which standing on the end came to the shoulder of a tall man. A variant and more fulsome account of this Indian description of Big Bone appears in Dr. Barton's *Archaeologiae Americanae Telluris Collectanea et Specimina, etc.*

9. *Archaeologiae Americanae Telluris Collectanea et Specimina or Collections with Specimens for a Series of Memoirs on Certain Extinct Animals and Vegetables of North America, etc.:* pp. 34-40. Philadelphia, 1814.
Various references to Big Bone Lick and its fossil mammoth, mastodon, and other extinct species. Shawnee description of Big Bone Lick given to Colonel Bouquette prior to 1762. Letters to Cuvier, Jefferson, and others. (U. S. G. S. Lib.)

BECKNER, LUCIEN

10. *John Findley: The First Pathfinder of Kentucky:* Vol. I, No. 3, p. 113. The History Quarterly of the Filson Club. Louisville, 1927.
Describes John Findley's trip to Big Bone Lick in the fall of 1752.

11. *Eskippakithiki: The Last Indian Town in Kentucky:* Vol. 6, p. 372. The Filson Club Quarterly. Louisville, 1932.
Cites John Findley's visit to Big Bone Lick in 1752, meeting there with Shawnee Indians and journey with them up Kentucky River to Eskippakithiki.

BELLIN, JACQUES NICOLAS

12. *Carte de La Louisiane, etc.:* Black and White, 22x15½ inches. Paris, 1744.
On this French map appears one of the first if not the first reference to the discovery of Big Bone Lick in these words: *"Endroit ou on a trouve des os d'Elephant en 1729."*

13. *Remarques sur le Carte de l'Amerique Septentrionale:* pp. 120-121. Paris, France, 1755.
   Refers to the French expedition down the Ohio in 1729, at which time de Longueil discovered Big Bone Lick. Bellin says here: "I am indebted for the topographical details of the course of this river to M. de Lery, Engineer, who surveyed it with the compass at the time that he descended it with a detachment of French [commanded by de Longueil] troops in 1729—"

BLUMENBACH, JOHANN FREDERICHS
14. *Handbuch der Naturgeschichte:* Gottingen, Germany, 1797. 1st ed. 1779, 3rd ed. 1788.
   The first determined species of the genus mastodon was from (Big Bone Lick) North America. Falconer. Pal. Men., etc., Vol. 1, p. 55, 1868. Blumenbach characterized this lesser proboscidian in 1797 as *Mammut Ohioticum,* hence M. Ohioticus. This is the first use of a specific name for this extinct mammal and precedes Cuvier's M. giganteus of 1805.

BODLEY, TEMPLE
15. *History of Kentucky:* Vol. I, p. 312. Chicago and Louisville, 1928.
   Indian scouts returning to the northern lake region reported to Captain Alexander McKee in the spring of 1782 that they "had discovered the enemy" (General Clark's "Big Knives") on their march below Big Bone Lick.

BONN, A. C.
16. *Verhandeling over de Mastodonte of Mammoth van den Ohio:* pp. 291-345, two plts. folded. Haarlem (Holland), 1809.
   Recites the discovery of Big Bone Lick by de Longueil. References to Croghan, Collinson, Hunter, Franklin, Shelbourne, Chappe, Michaelis, Peale, Cuvier, etc. (U. S. G. S. Lib.)

BROOKES, R.
17. *General Gazetteer—A New Geographical Dictionary:* Philadelphia and Richmond, 1812.
   Note on Big Bone Lick and its animal bones.

BROWN, A. C. (M. D.)
18. *Description of the Mastodon or Mammoth of Ohio:* Pamphlet. Amsterdam, 1809.
   States that George Croghan after visiting Big Bone Lick in 1765 removed some of the bones and sent them to Peter Collinson in London.

BIBLIOGRAPHY

BROWN, BARNUM

19. *A New Genus of Ground Sloth from the Pleistocene of Nebraska:* Bull. Amer. Mus. Nat. Hist., Vol. XIX, p. 571. New York, 1903.

States that "the type (fossil) Mylodon harlani taken from Big Bone Lick should be in Columbia University Museum but has been lost or mislaid." May have been destroyed in a fire in the old American Museum of Natural History. A cast of M. harlani is in the Museum at Williams College. (U. S. G. S. Lib.)

BUFFON, GEORGE LOUIS LECLERC DE

20. *Des Epoques de La Nature:* Vol. III, pp. 64-76. Plate, 9 figs. opp. p. 72. Paris, France, 1811. First ed., Paris, 1779.

Recites discovery of elephant teeth and tusks by George Croghan on the Ohio River at Big Bone Lick in 1765 and 1766 and makes comparisons. Cites Collinson. Figures nine views of mastodon teeth. (U. S. G. S. Lib.)

21. *Oeuvres completes De Buffon:* (Buffon et Daubenton, Lacepede, Cuvier, Dumerie, Poiret, Lesson et Geoffroy-St. Hilaire.) 6 Vol. (See Vol. II, pp. 33-38), Bruxelles, 1828 and 1829. Plates 1-6, Theorie de la Terre. Vol. I. Bruxelles, 1833.

Presents P. Collinson's letter of July 3, 1767, to Buffon. Gives credit for discovery of elephant bones in Canada (Big Bone Lick) to Croghan in the year 1765-1766 and figures teeth from those Croghan sent to him by Collinson, B. Franklin, Lord Shelbourne. Croghan's journal of 1765 excerpts. (U. S. G. S. Lib.)

BUFFON, GEORGE LOUIS LECLERC DE, AND OTHERS

22. *Histoir Naturelle, generale er particuliere:* (Sonnini) Vol. I, pp. 421-430, 3 pls.; Vol. IV, pp. 55-68, 3 pls. Paris, 1799.

Vol. I—General speculative discussion as to the fossil remains of great animals. Gives three plates showing mastodon molars. Refers to Canada. Buffon is said to have received bones from de Longueil about 1839 from Canada. Vol. IV. Presents P. Collinson's letter to Buffon of July 3, 1767, crediting discovery of Big Bone Lick to G. Croghan in 1765 and extract from Croghan's journal of same year. 3 plates of mastodon teeth collected at Big Bone in 1766 by Croghan.

BUTLER, MANN

23. *A History of the Commonwealth of Kentucky:* Pp. 368, 369. Louisville, 1834. Also second ed., 1836.

Reprints in the appendix the complete *Journal of Colonel Croghan*, beginning May 15, 1765, and telling of his visit to Big Bone Lick, May 30 and 31, 1765.

CARR, LUCIEN AND SHALER, N. S.
24. *On the Prehistoric Remains of Kentucky:* Kentucky Geological Survey, Mem. I, pt. 4, pp. 30-31. 1876.
"At Big Bone Lick the excavations have failed as yet to show a trace of man along with the extinct mammalia of the country. Altogether the indications are not in favor of a great antiquity of man in this district, but it is not yet time to form a final opinion on this point."

COLLINS, LEWIS
25. *History of Kentucky:* Pp. 180, 181. Maysville, 1850.
Historical descriptions of Big Bone Lick and its fossils. Cites James Douglas, Dr. Goforth, Thomas Ashe, Dr. Blake, President Jefferson, M. Cuvier, Mr. Finnell, and Mr. Graves. Cites sales of some fossil collections as high as $5,000.00.

COLLINS, RICHARD
26. *History of Kentucky:* Vol. I, pp. 15, 16, 17, 191, and 378; Vol. II, pp. 51, 52, 53, and 607. Covington, 1882.
Many historical and descriptive notes on Big Bone Lick and its fossils. M. de Longueil cited as discoverer of this lick in 1739. This is an error; M. de Longueil's discovery of Big Bone Lick was made in 1729. Also cites Christopher Gist, Robert Smith, George Croghan, Harry Gordon, Mary Ingles, Thomas Bullitt, Hancock Taylor, James, George, and Robert McAfee, and others.

COLLINSON, PETER
27. *On Some Very Large Fossil Teeth Found in North America:* (XLVI) Philosophical Transactions, Royal Society of London, original pub. Vol. LVII, p. 464 and p. 468, 1767. Reprint, Vol. XII, pp. 476-478, London, 1809. (See also Vol. VI, Sparks, Works of Benjamin Franklin, Boston, 1840.)
Discusses and describes "the elephants bones" collected by George Croghan, deputy of Sir William Johnson, the king's superintendent of Indian affairs in America at Big Bone Lick in 1766 and sent separately to Lord Shelbourne and Dr. Benjamin Franklin in London. (U. S. G. S. Lib.)
28. *Letter to George Buffon of July 3, 1767:* In Buffon's *Theorie de La Terre,* Vol. II, pp. 34-38. Bruxelles, 1829.
Tells of G. Croghan's visits to Big Bone Lick in 1765 and 1766. Gives portion of Croghan's journal of 1765. Buffon says nothing of receiving fossils from de Longueil in this complete work.

COLTON, HAROLD SELLERS
29. *Peale's Museum:* Pop. Sc. Monthly, Vol. 75, No. 3, pp. 221-238. September, 1909.

States: "Dr. Morgan gave him (Peale) some bones of a mammoth from Ohio" (Big Bone Lick) also that "the bones exhibited in Paris belong, I judge, to a mass of bones of several animals which were found at Big Bone Lick. (U. S. G. S. Lib.)

COOPER, CHALMER LEWIS

30. *Occurrence of Vertebrate Fossils in Kentucky:* Kentucky Geological Survey, Series VI, Vol. XXXVI, pp. 439-446.

Complete list of Big Bone Lick Mammalian Fauna; good Pleistocene bibliography.

COOPER, WILLIAM

31. *Two Young Skulls of an Extinct Animal Lately Found in Kentucky and New York Resembling the Mastodon:* Am. Jour. Sc., Vol. 19, No. 1, pp. 159-60. New Haven, October, 1830.

Refers to mastodon material from Kentucky (Big Bone Lick). (U. S. G. S. Lib.)

32. *Notices of Big Bone Lick:* Monthly Amer. Jour. of Geology, Vol. I, pp. 158-174, 205-216. 1831.

Gives a condensed history of the explorations made at Big Bone Lick for vertebrate fossils. An outline of all early collections and a list of the bones recovered together with the first estimate of the number of animals involved, possible methods of accumulation, geological notes, comparison with foreign depositories, specimens, etc. A very important early paper accompanied by the first published detailed map. (U. S. G. S. Lib.)

33. *A Report on Some Fossil Bones of the Megalonyx from Virginia, etc.:* Read January, 1833, Lyceum of Nat. History of New York, Vol. III, pp. 166-73. New York, 1836.

Numerous references and descriptions of Megalonyx material from Big Bone Lick. (U. S. G. S. Lib.)

COOPER, W., SMITH, J. A., AND DeKAY, J. E.

34. *Report of Messrs. Cooper, J. A. Smith, and DeKay to the Lyceum of Natural History, on a Collection of Fossil Bones disinterred at Big Bone Lick, Kentucky, in September, 1830, and recently brought to New York:* Am. Jour. Science, Vol. XX, pp. 370-372. 1831. Also Monthly Am. Journal of Geology, Vol. I, pp. 43-44. Philadelphia, 1831.

Describes the collection of Captain Benjamin Finnell. Cites it as containing specimens of the mastodon, mammoth, horse, buffalo, elk, moose, and ground sloth. Upwards of 300 bones in this collection besides 22 tusks, weight 5,300 pounds. It was shown in 1831 in New York City at the corner of Broadway and Pearl Sts. and was to be transferred to London or Paris. (U. S. G. S. Lib.)

COTTERILL, R. S.
35. *History of Pioneer Kentucky:* Pp. 9, 45. Cincinnati, 1917.
Describes Big Bone Lick in northern Kentucky as a sepulcher of the mastodon. Cites visitations to Big Bone of Gist in 1751.

COZZENS, ISSACHAN
35-A. *A Map of Big Bone Lick, Kentucky:* 1828, MSS. Original in New York Historical Society, New York City. Unpublished.
35-B. *A Map of Big Bone Lick, Kentucky:* 1830, MSS. with separate geological section. Original in New York Historical Society, New York City. Unpublished.

CRAMER, ZADOK
36. *The Navigator:* Pp. 41-42, Ed. 1806; pp. 69-70, Ed. 1808; pp. 117-120, Ed. 1811; pp. 114, 256-262, Ed. 1814; pp. 104, 225-230, Ed. 1817; pp. 101, 222-227, Ed. 1818; pp. 86, 201-206, Ed. 1824. Cramer, Spear, and Eichbaum, Pubs. Pittsburgh.
Description of Big Bone Lick. Letters of Caspar Wistar, Jun., and Dr. William Goforth relative to the Big Bone Lick fossils and the theft by Thomas Ashe of the Goforth collections in 1806-1807. Dr. Goforth states in his letters to President Thomas Jefferson in 1806 that he at one time had five tons of bones from Big Bone Lick.

CRESSWELL, NICHOLAS
37. *The Journal of Nicholas Cresswell, 1774-1777:* Pp. 76, 88, and 89. New York, 1928.
Passed Big Bone Creek travelling by canoe down the Ohio during the night of May 19-20, 1775. Returning visited Big Bone, Saturday, June 17, 1775. Interesting description.

CROGHAN, GEORGE
38. *Journey Down the Ohio in 1765:* Monthly American Journal of Geology and Natural Science. December, 1831.
The original manuscript by Croghan was acquired by George Featherstonhaugh, of Philadelphia, and published as above. This unique journal was reprinted by Mann Butler in his History of Kentucky in Louisville in 1834 and was reprinted again with fulsome notes in Early Western Travels Vol. I, by R. G. Thwaite, p. 135, in Cleveland in 1904. The Sir William Johnson version of this Journal appears in "New York Colonial Documents," vii, pp. 779-788. Another variant edition is printed in Hildreth's work "Pioneer History of the Ohio Valley."

CUMING, F.
39. *Sketches of a Tour to the Western Country:* Pp. 409-410. Pittsburgh, 1810. Reprinted in Early Western Travels: 1748-1846, R. G. Thwaite Ed., p. 257. Cleveland, 1904.

References to Big Bone Lick and a description of the Dr. Goforth collection of fossils taken from this locality and housed in Pittsburgh. (U. S. G. S. Lib.)

CUMMINGS, SAMUEL
40. *The Western Pilot, etc.:* Pp. 44 and 45. Cincinnati, 1834.
Gives notes on Big Bone Lick and repeats the impossible tradition of the Delaware Indians as related by Thomas Jefferson. Tells of Thomas Ashe taking several wagon loads of the bones to England. The 1825 edition of this book has a brief note on Big Bone Lick on page 19.

CUVIER, GEORGES DAGOBERT
41. *Memoires de l'Institut de France:* Ser. 1, Vol. II, pp. 1-22. Paris, 1796. (Lib. of Congress.)
A memoir on the various species of living and extinct elephants.
42. *Extrait d'un memoire sur les especes d'elephans vivantes et fossiles, par le citoyen Cuvier.* Jour. de Phys. Vol. 50, pp. 207-217. Paris, 1800.
Extract of a memoir on the species of living and fossil elephants. (Lib. of Congress.)
43. *Sur le Grand Mastodonte:* Annales du Museum D'Histoire Naturelle, Vol. 8, pp. 270-424. Paris, 1806. (Lib of Congress.)
44. *Sur les elephans vivans et fossiles:* Annales du Museum D'Histoire Naturelle, pp. 1-166, Vol. 8. Paris, 1806. (Lib. of Congress.)
45. *Recherches sur les Ossemens Fossiles:* Ed. 4, Vol. II, pp. 147, 148, 149, 253, 255, plates 21, 22, and 24. Paris, France, 1834; 1st ed. Paris, 1812.
Various notes as to Big Bone Lick, its discovery by De Longueil, its mammoth and mastodon bones and President Jefferson's gifts of fossil bones to the Institute of France. Bison latifrons from Big Bone Lick is here styled Aurochs. (U. S. G. S. Lib.)

D.................., J. F. N.
46. *A Compendium of the History of Canada, etc.:* Pp. xvi and 73. Montreal, 1874.
Cites De Longueil (Baron) as Governor and *ad* interim Governor of the colony of New France. De Longueil discovered Big Bone Lick in 1729.

DANIEL, FRANCOIS
47. *Le vicomte C. de Lery, lieutenent-general de l'Empire francais, ingenieur en chef de la grande armee, et sa famille:* Montreal, E. Senecal, 1867.
Civil and military achievements of M. Chaussegros de Lery who made the first compass survey of the Ohio River under the military

BIBLIOGRAPHY 133

escort of Charles Le Moyne de Longueil in 1729. De Lery family notes and references. (Lib. Congress.)

DARLINGTON, WILLIAM M.
48. *Christopher Gist's Journals, etc.:* Pp. 57, 58, and 129. **Pittsburgh,** 1893.
Reprints Gist's Journal with its reference to Big Bone Lick on March 13, and visit to this lick on March 18, 1751. Mentions Robert Smith and Hugh Crawford, also George Croghan, Peter Collinson, Dr. William Clarke of Cincinnati, and Thomas Jefferson.

DAVIS, DARRELL HAUG
49. *The Geography of the Blue Grass Region of Kentucky:* P. 160, Kentucky Geological Survey Series VI, Vol. 23. Frankfort, 1927.
Reference to Big Bone Lick as one of the three most celebrated Salt Licks in Kentucky.

EVANS, LEWIS
50. *A General Map of the Middle British Colonies in America:* 26x19⅜ inches. London and Philadelphia, 1755.
The first English map to note Big Bone Lick. It is inscribed "Elephant Bones found here" at the location of the famous salt lick near the Ohio River. From Big Bone a trail to the south and east is indicated and labeled "A War Path."

FALCONER, HUGH
51. *Palaeontological Memoirs and Notes:* Vol. I, Ed. by Charles Marchison, pp. 55-58. London, 1868.
An important chronologic outline of the early studies of the mastodon crediting it (*Mastodon Ohioticus*) to Big Bone Lick fossils first described by P. Collinson in Phil. Trans. in 1768.

FALCONER, HUGH, AND CANTLEY, P. I.
52. *Fauna Antiqua Sivalensis:* P. 136, Smith, Elder & Co. London, 1846. (Lib. U. S. Nat. Museum.)

FAXON, WALTER
53. *Relics of Peale's Museum:* Mus. Comp. Zool. Bull., Vol. 59, No. 3, pp. 117-148. Cambridge, Mass., July, 1915.
States (p. 125) Charles Wilson Peale's Philadelphia Museum had a modest beginning in 1784, with a paddle fish from the Alleghany River and some bones of a mastodon from the Ohio (Big Bone Lick). (U. S. G. S. Lib.)

FEATHERSTONHAUGH, GEORGE WILLIAM
54. *Scientific Memoranda:* Monthly American Jour. of Geology, Vol. I, pp. 42-43. Philadelphia, 1831.
Editorial note relative to report of the Lyceum of Natural History of New York by Cooper, Smith, and DeKay on Big Bone Lick fossils. (U. S. G. S. Lib.)

FILSON, JOHN
55. *The Discovery, Settlement, and Present State of Kentucke:* Pp. 32-36. Wilmington, 1784.
Big Bone Lick waters and their medicinal values are cited. The "big Bones" are described and the nature of the beasts from which they were derived is speculated upon.
56. *This Map of Kentucky, etc.:* Scale: 10 miles to an inch. 1st Ed. yellow border on hand laid paper with "PPD" water mark. Engraved by Henry D. Pursell and printed by T. Rook in Philadelphia, N. D. (1784).
This map locates Big Bone Lick as a "Salt and a Medicinal Spring on Big Bone Creek" where it is crossed by General Clarke's war road from Drennon Springs to the mouth of the Licking. It states, "the large bones are found here."

FITZROY, ALEXANDER
57. *The Discovery, Purchase, and Settlement of the Country of Kentuckie, etc.:* P. 13. London, 1786.
States at "a salt spring (Big Bone Lick) near the Ohio River, very large bones have been found."

FLOWER, W. H.
58. *Catalogue of Osteology and Dentition of Vertebrated Animals, Recent and Extinct:* Part II, Mammalia, p. 445. London, 1884.
Gives reference as to source of purchase and gift of the Big Bone Lick fossils in the Royal College of Surgeons in London, England.

FOOT, WILLIAM HENRY
59. *Sketches of Virginia: Historical and Biographical:* 2d series, pp. 150-159. Lippincott. Philadelphia, 1856.
Cites Mary Ingles' visitation to and escape from Big Bone Lick in 1756, while on a salt boiling expedition with a party of Shawnee Indians.

FRANKLIN, BENJAMIN
60. *Letter to George Croghan, London, August 5, 1767:* Pp. 275-276, in Vol. VI, Sparks' Works of Benjamin Franklin, Boston, 1840; also pp. 202-203 in Vol. 41, Ser. VI, Kentucky Geological Survey, Frankfort, 1931.
Discusses the "elephant's tusks and grinders" received through George Croghan from Big Bone Lick and gives his deductions concerning them. Dr. Franklin presented these bones to the Royal Society of London.
61. *Letter to Abbe Chappe, London, January 31, 1768:* P. 92 in Vol. 5 of Albert H. Smith's *Writings of Benjamin Franklin.*

BIBLIOGRAPHY 135

Franklin sends to Chappe, the great Siberian traveller, a proboscidian tooth from Big Bone Lick for comparison with those found in Siberia.

FUNKHOUSER, W. D.
62. *Wild Life in Kentucky:* Kentucky Geological Survey, Series VI, Vol. 16, pp. 30, 31, and 32. Frankfort, 1925.
Discusses prehistoric mammals of Kentucky and cites many found at Big Bone Lick.

GAZLEY, SAYRES (REV.)
63. *Notice of the Osseous Remains at Big Bone Lick, Kentucky:* (Art. XXV) Anonymous. Am. Jour. Sc., Vol. XVIII, pp. 139-141. New Haven, July, 1830.
A good early description by an eye witness of Big Bone Lick. Capt. Finnell "keeps the boarding house at this watering place." "The waters are beneficial to health; but the place is not much resorted to." (U. S. G. S. Lib.)

GILLELAND, J. C.
64. *Ohio and Mississippi Pilot, etc.:* P. 30. Pittsburgh, 1820.
Note as to Big Bone Lick on left side of the Ohio.

GIST, CHRISTOPHER
65. *Journal through Ohio and Kentucky in 1750 and 1751:* Ed. of William M. Darlington, pp. 57 and 58. Pittsburgh, 1893.
Describes his visit on Monday, March 18, 1851, to Big Bone Lick which he calls "the Lower Salt Lick." States that Robert Smith had said he visited Big Bone Lick 7 years previously and made collections of bones, that is in 1744.

GOODE, G. BROWN
66. *The Origin of the National Scientific and Educational Institutions of the United States:* P. 25 (Reprinted from the papers of the Am. Hist. Assn.). G. P. Putnam's Sons. New York, 1890.
Cites Thomas Jefferson's interest in paleontology particularly as exemplified by his personal collection from Big Bone Lick. (Lib. Nat. Museum.)

GORDON, HARRY (CAPTAIN)
67. *A Journey Down the Ohio in 1766:* Public Archives of Canada, Shelbourne MSS., Vol. 48, pp. 159-178. Copy. Copied by J. Coussens. Endorsed: "Copy of Capt. Gordon's Journal. 1766. Enclosed in General Gage's letter (No. 5) of the 22nd of February, 1767."

In this journal Captain Gordon tells of his visit to Big Bone Lick in 1766 and describes the locality. It was at this time that collections were made for Lord Shelbourne and Benjamin Franklin.

GRAHAM, EDWARD
68. *Letter to John Breckenridge, September 25, 1795:* Breckinridge MSS., MS. Division, Library of Congress. Washington, 1795.

Proposes the establishment of a museum of natural history at Lexington, Kentucky, with a mammoth skeleton from Big Bone Lick as the central nucleus.

GRAY, BEULAH B.
69. *The National Lincoln Memorial Highway Over the Buffalo Trace:* 80 pp. 1931.

Outlines the old Buffalo trace from the prairies of central Illinois to the Wabash River at Vincennes, thence to the Falls of the Ohio into Kentucky, to Big Bone Lick and eastwardly.

HALE, J. P.
70. *Trans Allegheny Pioneers:* Pp. 29-30. Cincinnati, 1886.

Describes Mary Ingles captivity by the Shawnees and visit to Big Bone in 1756.

HANNA, C. A.
71. *The Wilderness Trail:* Pp. 42, 117, 126, 127, 157, 238, 242, 245, 247, and 249. G. P. Putnam's Sons. New York, 1912.

Many references to Big Bone Lick. Citation of French expedition conducted with troops by M. Chaussegros de Lery, an engineer, in 1729. His compass survey of the Ohio and topographical notes formed the basis of N. Bellin's map of 1744. See pp. 126-127 and copy of N. Bellin's map.

HANSON, THOMAS
72. *Journal Kept on the River Ohio in the Year 1774:* P. 121, in Thwaites and Kellogg's *Dunmore's War.* Madison, 1905.

Describes John Floyd's survey on May 12, 1774, of 1,000 acres including Big Bone Lick for Col. William Christian.

HARLAN, RICHARD
73. *Fauna Americana: being a description of the mammaliferous animals inhabitating North America:* Pp. 272-273. A. Finley. Philadelphia, 1825.

Describes the portion of a skull of an extinct fossil bison originally presented to the American Philosophical by Samuel Brown of Kentucky. This specimen had previously been described by Rembrandt Peale in 1803. Harlan names the specie *Bos latifrons.* This specimen came from near Big Bone Lick. Dr. Leidy later renamed it *Bison latifrons.*

BIBLIOGRAPHY 137

74. *Description of the Fossil Bones of the Megalonyx Discovered in "White Cave," Kentucky:* Jour. Acad. Nat. Sci., Phila., Vol. VI, Part I, pp. 277, 279, 284. Philadelphia, 1829.

Descriptions and references to the humerous of a megalonyx disinterred at Big Bone Lick. (Lib. U. S. Nat. Museum and U. S. G. S. Lib.)

75. *Description of the Jaws, Teeth, and Clavicle of the Megalonyx Laqueatus:* Monthly Amer. Jour. Geol., Vol. I, pp. 74-76, pl. III, figs. 1 to 3 (1831).

Describes a left ramus of the lower jaw of a ground sloth and calls it *Megalonyx laqueatus*. Later shown by Owen to be *Mylodon harlani*. This specimen was once a part of the Finnell collection in Cincinnati and came (according to Jos. Leidy, 1855) from Big Bone Lick. (U. S. G. S. Lib.)

HAY, OLIVER P.

76. *The Pleistocene Period and Its Vertebrata:* Pp. 539-784, 36th annual report. Dept. of Geology and Natural Resources of Indiana.

Many descriptions and references to Pleistocene fossils from Big Bone Lick.

77. *The Pleistocene of North America, etc.:* Pub. No. 322, pp. 43, 128, 146, 160, 181, 202, 209, 234, 243, 255, 265, 270, 401-405, Carnegie Institution of Washington. Washington, D. C., 1923.

A summary statement of the vertebrate paleontology of Big Bone Lick, together with numerous separate descriptions of occurrence of individual genera.

HAYS, ISAAC

78. *Descriptions of the Inferior Maxillary Bones of Mastodons in the Cabinet of the American Philosophical Society, etc.:* Extract from Trans. of the Am. Phil. Soc., Vol. IV, N. S. Philadelphia, 1833.

Numerous references to fossils from Big Bone Lick. (U. S. G. S. Lib.)

HODGSON, WILLIAM B.

79. *Memoir on the Megatherium, etc.:* 47 pp., 1 map, 1 sect., 1 plt. New York, 1846.

Refers (p. 7) to discovery of fossil bones at Big Bone Lick. (U. S. G. S. Lib.)

HOLMES, FRANCIS S.

80. *Post-Pliocene Fossils of South Carolina:* Pp. 104, 106, 107, pl. XVI, figs. 7, 8. Charleston, 1860.

In this Joseph Leidy describes and figures the tooth of a tapier (Tapirus haysii) said to have come from Big Bone Lick. (Lib. Nat. Museum.)

HUNTER, WILLIAM

81. *Observations on the Bones, commonly supposed to be Elephant's Bones, which have been found near the River Ohio in America.* Phil. Trans., Royal Soc. of London, Vol. LVIII, p. 34, 1768, and reprinted, Vol. XII, pp. 504-507, London, 1809.

Observations on the mastodon fossils from Big Bone Lick sent to Lord Shelbourne and Dr. Franklin. Figured and compared with elephant in plate XV, and this the first published reproduction of a fossil from Big Bone Lick. (U. S. G. S. Lib.)

HUTCHINS, THOMAS

82. *A New Map of the Western Parts of Virginia, Pennsylvania, Maryland, and North Carolina, etc.:* London, 1778. Reprinted by F. C. Hicks. Cleveland, 1904.

Hutchins visited Big Bone Lick with Capt. Harry Gordon in 1766. He locates the lick on the above map by simply using the words "Big Bones."

83. *A Topographical description of Virginia, Pennsylvania, Maryland, and North Carolina:* London, 1778. In reprint by F. C. Hicks, pp. 82 and 83. Cleveland, 1904.

Describes the Big Bone Lick as "Several large and miry Salt Springs." Refers to Dr. Hunter's observations.

IMLAY, CAPT. GILBERT

84. *Topographical Description of the Western Territory of North America:* Pp. 47-48; p. 236 and p. 304, J. Debrett. London, 1793.

Locates "Great Bone Lick" geographically and discusses the possible origin of the bones. Reference to Buffon, Jefferson, Hunter, and Cline.

JEFFERSON, THOMAS

85. *Notes on the State of Virginia:* Pp. 78-89. Philadelphia, June, 1801.

Gives reference to Big Bone Lick and describes the size and nature of extinct animals represented by the fossils collected there. First publication (pp. 79-80) of Indian legend as to last of the mastodons at Big Bone Lick. Important paper. (U. S. G. S. Lib.)

86. *Letter to Dr. Caspar Wistar, Washington, February 25, 1807:* Pp. 158-159 in Vol. XI of the Writings of Thomas Jefferson. Washington, 1904.

Encloses letter of Dr. Goforth relative to the Big Bone Lick fossils. Outlines his plan to have Captain William Clarke "stop at the lick" and make collections for him at his own expense. Proposes to give these specimens without cost to the American Philosophical Society.

87. *Letter to General George Rogers Clarke, Washington, December 19, 1807:* P. 406 in Vol. XI, Writings of Thomas Jefferson. Washington, 1904.

Requests that balance of bones from Big Bone Lick be packed and sent to him through William Brown, collector, of the port of New Orleans. Then follows a personal remembrance to General Clarke.

88. *Letter to General William Clarke, Washington, December 19, 1807:* Pp. 404-405 in Vol. XI, Writings of Thomas Jefferson. Washington, 1904.

Refers to General Clarke's letters to him of September 20th and November 10th, relative to the collections of fossils made at Big Bone Lick and asks that other specimens stored at the residence of General George Rogers Clarke at Clarksville be also forwarded to him at Washington, via New Orleans.

89. *Letter to Doctor Caspar Wistar, Washington, December 19, 1807:* Pp. 403-404 in Vol. XI, Writings of Thomas Jefferson. Washington, 1904.

Discusses the work of fossil collecting of General William Clarke at Big Bone Lick and the type of fossils recovered and forwarded to Washington. Indicates his desire to send a few "to the National Institute of France." Invites Wistar to Washington to be his guest.

90. *Letter to Doctor Caspar Wistar, Washington, March 20, 1808:* Pp. 15 and 16 in Vol. XII, Writings of Thomas Jefferson. Washington, 1904.

Invites Dr. Wistar to visit him at the White House and inspect his collection of "Upwards of three hundred bones" made for the President by General William Clarke at Big Bone Lick.

91. *Letter to General William Clarke, Monticello, September 10, 1809:* Pp. 309-310 in Vol. XII, Writings of Thomas Jefferson. Washington, 1904.

Refers to the additional 3 boxes of bones sent from Big Bone Lick to him through Mr. Brown of New Orleans, and says that the bill of lading was received but that the bones were put off at St. Mary's near Havana. He is at a loss to know what was done with these bones.

JILLSON, WILLARD ROUSE

92. *Geological Research in Kentucky:* Pp. 120 and 121, Kentucky Geological Survey, Series VI, Vol. 15. Frankfort, 1923.

Gives titles of book and pamphlets referring to Big Bone Lick.

BIBLIOGRAPHY

93. *The Kentucky Land Grants:* P. 37, The Filson Club Publications No. 33. Louisville, 1925.

    Cites William Christian's 1,000-acre grant from Virginia on the Ohio River of May 16, 1774, as in Book 5, p. 23. This is the John Floyd Survey of Big Bone Lick.

94. *Old Kentucky Entries and Deeds:* Pp. 200, 444, and 478, Filson Club Publications No. 34. Louisville, 1926.

    Indexes the entry of James Douglas to 500 acres at Big Bone Lick on May 22, 1780; also the deed of 1,000 acres of land including Big Bone Lick from Colonel William Christian to David Ross, December 22, 1780.

95. *Geology and Mineral Resources of Kentucky:* Pp. 19 and 20, Kentucky Geological Survey, Series VI, Vol. 17. Frankfort, 1928.

    Cites Big Bone Lick as one of the most ancient and celebrated mineral springs. Geology of Boone County presented.

96. *Sketch of the Life of John Filson* in *Filson's Kentucke:* P. 140, The Filson Club Publications No. 35. Louisville, 1929.

    Refers to the land owned in 1783 by John Filson on Big Bone Lick Creek in Boone County, Kentucky.

97. *Geologic Map of Kentucky:* Scale; 1:500,000. Kentucky Geological Survey, Series VI. Frankfort, 1929.

    Shows areal geology of Big Bone Lick and inclusion within the southern limit of the drift of the Illinoian advance of the continental ice sheet.

98. *Pleistocene Proboscidians within the Cumberland Plateau in Kentucky:* Bull. Geol. Soc. America, Vol. 40, No. 1, p. 253. 1929.

    Refers to recent discoveries of mastodon teeth in Jackson and Magoffin Counties in Eastern Kentucky.

99. *The Paleontology of Kentucky:* Pp. v and xi, 38-41, and 439-447, Kentucky Geological Survey, Series VI, Vol. 36. Frankfort, 1931.

    The best group of summary statements as to the discovery of Big Bone Lick and its systematic paleontology in the literature of Kentucky.

100. *Structural Geologic Map of Kentucky:* Scale; 1:500,000; 100-foot contours, Kentucky Geological Survey, Series VI. Frankfort, 1931.

    Shows regional structural geology of Big Bone Lick area and proximity to top of Cincinnati arch.

101. *The Kentuckie Country:* P. 41. Washington, D. C., 1931.

    Reprints in facsimile Fitzroy's, "Discovery, Purchase, and Settlement of the Country of Kentuckie," and with it his notes on Big Bone Lick. Also the "Whatman" edition of John Filson's *Map of Kentucke* of 1784, showing location of Big Bone Lick.

BIBLIOGRAPHY 141

102. *An Introduction to Kentucky Paleontology:* Pp. xi and xii of Vol. 36, The Paleontology of Kentucky, Kentucky Geological Survey, Series VI. Frankfort, 1931.
Early explorations of Big Bone Lick are cited in chronological order.

103. *Paleontological Beginnings in Kentucky:* Pan-American Geologist, Vol. LVII, pp. 38-44. Des Moines, February, 1932.
This is a reprinting of the previous title *An Introduction, etc.* It sets out the succession of explorative visitations to Big Bone Lick.

104. *The Ohio Country: A Colonial Historical Sketch:* P. 12, Society of Colonial Wars in the State of Ohio. Cincinnati, 1932.
Cites De Celeron's journey down the Ohio in 1749.

105. *Kentuckie—A Colonial Narrative:* P. 11. Louisville, 1932.
Cites De Longueil's discovery of Big Bone Lick and the remains of the mammoth.

106. *Early Kentucky Maps:* Unpublished MSS., p. 28. 1933.
The first record of Big Bone Lick is found on N. Bellin's Carte de la Louisiane, etc., of 1744 which states the bones of the elephant were found there in 1729.

107. *Pioneer Kentucky:* Pp. 9, 36, 109, 111, 117, End sheet decorations and page sketch map of Kentucky. Frankfort, 1934.
States Big Bone Lick was discovered by the French in 1729; location, notes, and references. Map on page 36 locates Big Bone Lick.

108. *The Big Bones of Northern Kentucky:* Register, Kentucky State Historical Society, Vol. 33, No. 104, pp. 181-190, two map pls. Frankfort, July, 1935.
An address covering the principal historical, paleontological, and geological features of Big Bone Lick delivered at the Hotel Sinton, Cincinnati, Ohio, May 22, 1935.

JODOIN, ALEX.

109. *Histoire de Longueuil et de la famille de Longueuil:* Par Alex. Jodoin, et J. L. Vincent. Montreal, Impr. Gebhardt-Berthiaume, 1889.
Family history of the De Longueils in Canada. Charles Le Moyne de Longueil commanding the military escort of the De Lery expedition surveying the Ohio discovered Big Bone Lick according to Nicolas Bellin, French Carbographer in 1729. (Lib. Congress.)

JOHNSTON, J. STODDARD

110. *First Explorations of Kentucky:* The Filson Club. Pubs. No. 13, pp. 149-151. Louisville, 1898.

Reprints Christopher Gist's Journal of 1750-1751 and his several references to Big Bone Lick at that time.

111. *The Fauna of Kentucky:* Pp. 47-48, The Western Farmers' Almanac. Louisville, 1909.

References to Big Bone Lick and its glacial fauna.

KERR, CHARLES (Editor)

112. *History of Kentucky:* Vol. I, pp. 72, 84, 160, 532. Chicago and New York, 1922.

C. Gist's interest in Big Bone Lick and description. Robert Smith's visit in 1744 cited. Mary Ingles' visitation in 1756. Arnold Viele probably in Kentucky in 1693. Big Bone Lick found and described in 1729. Edward Graham writes John Breckenridge in 1795 and proposes a museum of natural history in Lexington to display with other things the skeleton of a mammoth from Big Bone Lick.

KINDLE, EDWARD M.

113. *The Story of the Discovery of Big Bone Lick:* Kentucky Geological Survey, Series VI, Vol. 31, pp. 189-212. Frankfort, 1931.

Describes the visit of George Croghan in 1765 and Harry Gordon in 1766. Refers to the interest of Benjamin Franklin in 1767, also to the work of O. P. Hay and N. S. Shaler. Photos of restorations of mastodon and Big Bone Lick. References to Charles Lyell's visit in 1841-42.

KINKEAD, LUDIE J., AND HEALY, KATHARINE G.

114. *Calendar of Bond and Power of Attorney Book, No. 1, Jefferson County, Kentucky, 1783-1798:* Part One, pp. 41-42, The Filson Club Quarterly, Vol 7. Louisville, 1933.

Agreement between Robert Daniel and Richard Jones Waters both of Jefferson County by which Daniel is to sell 1,000 acres of land on Ohio River near Big Bone at rate of £25 per 100 acres, Virginia currency.

LEAHY, ETHEL C.

115. *Who's Who on the Ohio River and Its Tributaries:* Pp. 156, 157, 158, and 159. Cincinnati, 1931.

Reprints Cramer's *Navigator* of 1914 and its descriptions of Big Bone Lick; also the Wistar, Goforth, and Jefferson correspondence of 1806.

LEIDY, JOSEPH

116. *On the Fossil Horse of America:* Proc. Acad. Nat. Sci. of Phila., Vol. III, pp. 263 and 264, 1847. Philadelphia, 1848.

Description of ten molar teeth of the fossil horse taken from Big Bone Lick and presented to the Academy by Mr. J. P. Wetherill. (U. S. G. S. Lib.)

117. *Bison Antiquus:* Proc. Acad. Nat. Sci., p. 140, 1851; p. 117. Philadelphia, 1852.

This is the first description of Bison antiquus and was made from a fragment of horncore and skull from Big Bone Lick, collected by General Clark for Thomas Jefferson.

118. *On the Extinct Species of American Ox:* (From Smithsonian Contrib. to Know., Vol. 5) 20 pp., 5 pls. Philadelphia, 1852.

Many systematic references to the Pleistocene oxen or bison recovered from Big Bone Lick. A very important paper.

119. *Remarks on the Question of the Identity of Bootherium carifrons with Oribos mashatus or o. maximus:* Proc. Acad. of Nat. Sci. of Phila., Vol. VII, pp. 209-210. Philadelphia, 1856.

Reply in dispute with Sir John Richardson as to proper identification of Bootherium taken from Big Bone Lick.

120. *The Extinct Mammalian Fauna of Dakota and Nebraska with a Synopsis of Extinct Mammalia of North America:* 30 pls., 472 pp. Philadelphia, 1869.

A very important contribution. See Bib. pp. 373, 374, 375, 392, 393, 394, 395, 396, 397, 398, 399, 400, 411, 413, etc. Many references to paleontological literature of Big Bone Lick. (U. S. Nat. Museum Lib. Also Lib. of Cong.)

121. *Report on American Mastodon Remains in Warren Museum and Cambridge University Museum:* Proc. Acad. Nat. Sci. of Phila., p. 97. Philadelphia, 1870.

Brief description of mastodon, elephant, bison, horse, musk ox, and other vertebrate fossils from Big Bone Lick collected by Prof. Shaler who informed him "that he had detected no evidence of glacial action" there. (U. S. G. S. Lib.)

LEVERETT, FRANK

122. *The Pleistocene of Northern Kentucky:* Pp. 77-80, Kentucky Geological Survey, Series VI, Vol. 31. Frankfort, 1929.

Numerous geological references to Big Bone Lick. Reprints of excerpts from Filson (1784) and Imlay (1793) relating to Big Bone.

123. *Glacial Formations and Drainage Features of the Erie and Ohio Basins:* Monogr. U. S. G. S., Vol. XLI, pp. 257-8. Washington, 1902.

Discusses physiographic features produced by Illinoian ice sheet in the vicinity of Big Bone Lick.

124. *Big Bone Lick, and Early Views as to Fossils Found There:* (Appendix II) pp. 77-80 in The Pleistocene of Northern Kentucky, Kentucky Geological Survey, Series VI, Vol. 31. Frankfort, 1929.

Reprints of the Filson (1784) and the Imlay (1793) descriptions of Big Bone Lick. Leverett perpetrates through O. P. Hay the error of the first visit and collection (by M. de Longueil) in 1739. The correct date of this visit by M. de Longueil was 1729. Cites John Filson, William Henry Harrison; gives list of Big Bone fossils.

LEVERETT, FRANK, AND TAYLOR, F. B.

125. *The Pleistocene of Indiana and Michigan and the History of the Great Lakes:* U. S. Geological Survey, Mon. 53, p. 62. Washington, 1915.

Outlines the border of Illinoian drift as covering the Big Bone Lick map.

LLOYD, JOHN URI

126. *When Did the American Mammoth and Mastodon Become Extinct?* Pp. 43-46, Records of the Past, Vol. III, Part II. Washington, February, 1904. Variant in Purple and Gold of the Burlington, Ky., H. S., pp. 7-9, with photo of author. Burlington, 1916.

Discusses antiquity of the mammoth and the mastodon at Big Bone Lick, concluding that these species persisted in this locality until a very short time, perhaps a century or so, before white men first arrived. Indian tradition is given.

LUCAS, F. A.

127. *The Fossil Bison of North America:* Proc. U. S. Nat. Mus., Vol. XXI, No. 1172, pp. 755-771, pl. LXV-LXXXIV. 1899.

Systematically arranges, describes, and figures the various types of American bison; cites Bison bison, Bison antiquus, and Bison latifrons occurring as type fossils at Big Bone Lick.

LYDEKKER, RICHARD

128. *Catalogue of the Fossil Mammalia in the British Museum:* Pt. 2, p. 27. London, 1885.

Cites No. 40847 as a fragment of a right mandible of *Bison latifrons* from Pleistocene from Big Bone Lick. (Lib. Nat. Museum.)

129. *Catalogue of the Fossil Mammalia in the British Museum:* Pt. IV, pp. 17, 19, 20, 21, 22, 23, 24, 25. London, 1886.

Cites many complete and fragmental mammoth and mastodon bones, teeth, and tusks in this collection from Big Bone Lick beginning with Croghan-Gordan collection of 1766 which was presented by the Earl of Shelbourne, in 1768. (Lib. Nat. Museum.)

BIBLIOGRAPHY 145

LYELL, SIR CHARLES
130. *Travels in North America, 1841-42:* Murray ed., Vol. II, pp. 53-59. New York, 1845. Subsequent editions in English and German.
Describes Big Bone Lick and the area adjoining. Speculates on the order of superposition of the various glacial mammals found here. Cites physiography, geology, vertebrate and invertebrate paleontology.

131. *On the Geological Position of Mastodon Giganteum and Associated Fossil Remains at Big Bone Lick, Kentucky, etc.:* Am. Jour. Science, Vol. 46, pp. 320-323, 1844; Geol. Soc. London, Proc., Vol. 4, No. 92, 1844.
Briefly describes geography, topography, geology, and mode of occurrence of fossil bones at Big Bone Lick. Lyell states it plainly as a fact, but of course erroneously, that glacial drift did not cover this area. Says buffalo paths still to be seen there. (U. S. G. S. Lib.)

MACLEAN, J. P.
132. *Mastodon, Mammoth, and Man:* 84 pp., Illus., 2d Ed., R. Clark. Cincinnati, 1880.
Recites discovery of Big Bone Lick by De Longueil (p. 13) but incorrectly states that he collected bones of the mastodon and returning to Paris presented them to D'Aubenton and Buffon. (U. S. G. S. Lib.)

MARSHALL, HUMPHREY
133. *History of Kentucky:* Vol. 1, pp. 17, 38. Frankfort, 1824.
References to Big Bone Lick and pre-historic animals. Cites De Longueil's discovery (in 1729) of the lick erroneously as 1739. This evidently was Collins' source of statement and error.

MATLOCK, TIMOTHY
134. *A Large Tusk Found in the Back Country:* Trans. Am. Phil. Soc. of Phila., Vol. 22, p. 193. Philadelphia, 1885.
May have been from Big Bone. Was read and two pieces of the tusk exhibited on March 18, 1791, in Philadelphia.

McAFEE, ROBERT
135. *Journal of an Exploration through Kentucky in 1773:* Pp. 433 and 445. Pub. in the Woods-McAfee Memorial by N. M. Woods. Louisville, 1905.
Describes the appearance of Big Bone Lick on July 4, 1773, when Robert and James McAfee, Thomas Bullitt, and others visited the locality. Notes are appended.

McELROY, ROBERT McNUTT
136. *Kentucky in the Nation's History:* P. 12. New York, 1909.
Footnotes as to George Croghan's visit to Big Bone in 1765.

M'MURTRIE, H. (M. D.)
137. *Sketches of Louisville:* Pp. 82-83. Louisville, 1819.
States: "These gigantic remains have been chiefly taken from Big Bone Lick—" A list of the fossils removed from Big Bone by Dr. Mitchell upon the order of Governor Clark is presented.

MEISEL, MAX
138. *A Bibliography of American Natural History, 1769-1865:* Vol. II. 1926.
Many references to early scientific papers on fossils recovered from Big Bone Lick. (U. S. G. S. Lib.)

MERCER, H. C.
139. *The Lenape Stone:* Pp. 12-15, G. P. Putnam's Sons. New York, 1885.
Cites the fact that "the great bones (at Big Bone Lick) often seemed hardly older than those of modern animals with which they were mingled—." Discusses the contemporaneity of the mammoth and the Indian in North America.

MERRILL, GEORGE P.
140. *Contributions to the History of American Geology:* P. 213, Report of U. S. National Museum. Washington, 1904.
References to Big Bone Lick and Thomas Jefferson as a paleontologist in the White House in 1797.

141. *The First Hundred Years of American Geology:* P. 16. New Haven, 1924.
Refers to Thomas Jefferson as a paleontologist and his collection of more than 300 specimens of fossil bones brought to the White House at his own expense from Big Bone Lick.

MILLER, ARTHUR McQUISTON
142. *The Geology of Kentucky:* Kentucky Geological Survey, Series V, Vol. II, p. 220. Frankfort, 1919.
Discusses Big Bone Lick and states first account of this lick was made by M. de Longueil, a Frenchman, who visited the locality in 1739. This is a perpetuation of Richard Collins' error. M. de Longueil discovered Big Bone Lick in 1729. Also cities Gist and Buffon.

BIBLIOGRAPHY 147

143. *Licks and Caves of the Lower Ohio Valley as Repositories of Mammalian Remains Including Those of Man:* Bull. Geol. Soc. of America, 33, No. 1. 1922.
    References to fossil remains at Big Bone Lick.

MITCHELL, SAMUEL L.
144. *Observations on the Geology of North America, etc.:* Pp. 361-362, pub. with Essay on the Theory of the Earth (Cuvier), and other items. New York, 1818.
    References to Big Bone Lick and its fossil bones. (Lon. Pub. Lib. and U. S. G. S. Lib.)
145. *Catalogue of the Organic Remains and Other Geological and Mineralogical Articles contained in the Collection Presented to the New York Lyceum of Natural History:* P. 11. New York, 1826.
    Cites several mastodon bones and tusks from Kentucky, probably disinterred at Big Bone Lick. (U. S. G. S. Lib.)

MORSE, JEDIDIAH
146. *The American Universal Geography:* P. 499 (6th ed.). Boston, 1819.
    Reference to Big Bone Lick.

OSBORN, HENRY FAIRFIELD
147. *The Age of Mammals:* Pp. 478, 480, 482, 487, 492, Macmillan. New York, 1910.
    Numerous references to Big Bone Lick and its vertebrate fauna.
148. *Thomas Jefferson as a Paleontologist:* Science, Vol. 82, No. 2136, pp. 533-538, December 6, 1935.
    Many references to Big Bone Lick and Jefferson's interest therein as evidenced by his correspondence which is reprinted.

OWEN, RICHARD
149. *Zoology of the Voyage of H. M. S. Beagle, 1832-1836:* Part I, Fossil Mammalia, p. 68. London, 1840.
    References to *Megalonyx laqueatus* as described by Dr. Harlan from Big Bone Lick. (Lib. of Cong.)

PEALE, REMBRANDT
150. *Account of the Skeleton of the Mammoth a Non-descript Carnivorous Animal of Immense Size Found in America:* 46 pp. London, 1802.
    Refers to discovery of "great numbers of bones" at Big Bone Lick (p. 8). An important contribution. (U. S. G. S. Lib.)
151. *Account of Some Remains of a Species of Gigantic Oxen Found in America and Other Parts of the World:* Philosophical Mag., Vol. XV, pp. 325-327, pl. vi. Philadelphia, 1803.

Describes the fragment of a bison skull sent to the American Philosophical Society by Samuel Brown from a locality near Big Bone Lick. This specimen later described by George Cuvier, Richard Harlan, and others. It was the first fossil Bison found and described in America. Harlan named it *Bos Latifrons*.

152. *An Historical Disquisition on the Mammoth or Great American Incognitum, etc.*: 81 pp., 1 pl. London, 1803.

    Credits in preface "some of the first discovered bones of the mammoth," from Big Bone Lick given to his father, Charles Wilson Peale by Dr. Brown as responsible for the establishment in 1785 of Peale's Philadelphia Museum, the first museum in America. Many references to Big Bone Lick. This is an expansion of his *Account of the Skeleton*, etc., of 1802. (U. S. G. S. Lib.)

PERRIN, W. H., BATTLE, J. H., AND KNIFFIN, G. C.

153. *Kentucky—A History of the State:* Pp. 115 and 549-550. Louisville and Chicago, 1886; pp. 655-656 in ed. of 1888.

    A running account of the discovery and early collection of "big bones" at Big Bone Lick taken principally from Cramer's *Navigator* and Collins' *History of Kentucky*. Rafinesque's original (1824) error as to the date of De Longueil's discovery of Big Bone is perpetrated. Robert McAfee, Dr. William Goforth, Thomas Ashe, Dr. Blake, Prof. Monroe, Thomas Jefferson, George Cuvier, Mr. Finnell are cited.

POWNALL, THOMAS

154. *A Topographical Description of Such Parts of North America, etc.*: London, 1776.

    Contains a portion of the Journal of Captain Harry Gordon, kept on his journey down the Ohio from Fort Pitt to Illinois. On this journey in 1766 he stopped at Big Bone Lick. This volume also contains a printing of Col. Christopher Gist's journal of an expedition through Kentucky in 1751 at which time he visited and collected a large tooth from Big Bone Lick.

PURCELL, MARTHA GRASHAM

155. *Stories of Old Kentucky:* Pp. 27-28. New York, 1915.

    Reviews the visitations of James Douglas to Big Bone Lick in 1773 and describes the occurrence of the bones of the mastodon and mammoth.

RAFINESQUE, C. S.

156. *Ancient Annals of Kentucky:* P. 17, in Marshall's History of Kentucky, Vol. I. Frankfort, 1824.

BIBLIOGRAPHY 149

References to Big Bone Lick, De Longueil's discovery is misstated as 1739. It should have been 1729. This is perhaps the beginning of this notable error of date.

157. *Visit to Big Bone Lick in 1821:* Monthly Am. Jour. of Geology and Natural Science, Vol. I, No. 8, pp. 355-358. Philadelphia, February, 1832.

   An interesting early description of Big Bone Lick. John D. Clifford. Indian mound near this Lick. (U. S. G. S. Lib.)

RICHARDSON, ANDREW

158. *A Short Description of the Bones of the Mammoth, etc., Found in Big Bone Lick, Ken., etc.:* Cramer's Pittsburgh Magazine Almanack. Pittsburgh, 1805.

   An abbreviated list of Big Bone Lick fossils collected by Dr. William Goforth.

ROTHERT, OTTO A. (Editor)

159. *Big Bone Lick:* Vol. 4, p. 127; Vol. 5, p. 197, The Filson Club Quarterly. Louisville, 1930 and 1931.

   Reference to McAfee visitation in 1773 to Big Bone Lick.

RULE, LUCIEN V.

160. *John D. Shane's Interview with Ephraim Sandusky:* Vol. 8, pp. 220-221, The Filson Club Quarterly. Louisville, 1934. Original in IICC, 141-45 Kentucky Papers, Draper MSS., Wisconsin State Hist. Soc. Madison, Wisconsin.

   Describes early salt making (1797-8-9) at Big Bone Lick by David Ross, Thomas Carneal, Davis Carneal, Jacob Sowdusky (Sandusky). Sea trip from New Orleans to New York and Big Bone narrative en route.

SHALER, NATHANIEL SOUTHGATE

161. *Preliminary Note* to the *American Bisons:* Memoir, Kentucky Geological Survey, Vol. 1, part I, p. iii. Cambridge, 1876.

   Introductory references to J. A. Allen's *American Bisons* and the Big Bone Lick fossils discussed therein.

162. *On the Age of the Bison in the Ohio Valley:* Memoir, Vol. 1, part II, pp. 232-236. Cambridge, 1876.

   Discusses the sequence of *Bison latifrons* and *Bison americaness* and other glacial animals at Big Bone Lick based upon excavations made in 1868 and 1869.

163. *(Big Bone Lick)* Kentucky Geological Survey, Reports of Progress, Series II, Vol. III, Chapter III, pp. 66-69, and p. 197. Frankfort, 1877.

BIBLIOGRAPHY

    Describes his exploration at Big Bone Lick in 1868, gives list of fossils recovered and cites order of succession. Gives his views as to age of big bone accumulation, etc.

164. *Kentucky—A Pioneer Commonwealth:* Pp. 41 and 42. Boston and New York, 1884.

    A general geological description of Big Bone Lick and its fossils.

165. *The Autobiography of Nathaniel Southgate Shaler:* Pp. 247-248. Boston and New York, 1909.

    Reference to Professor Shaler's excavations at Big Bone Lick in 1868.

SHIDELER, W. H.

166. *Geologic Map of Boone County, Kentucky:* Scale; 1:62,500. Colors pink, yellow, blue, and black; Kentucky Geological Survey, Series VI. Frankfort, 1931.

    Shows detailed areal geology of the region around Big Bone Lick.

SILLIMAN, BENJAMIN

167. *Remarks by the Editor:* American Journal of Science, Vol. XX, pp. 371-372. New Haven, 1831.

    Says after seeing the exhibit from Big Bone Lick shown in New York City: "They (the bones) produced in the beholder the strongest conviction that races of animals formerly existed on this continent, not only of vast magnitude, but which also must have been very numerous; and the Mastodon, at least, ranged in herds, over probably the entire American continents." (U. S. G. S. Lib.)

SMITH, WILLIAM BAILEY

168. *Letter to Col. George Rogers Clark, from Holston River, March 29, 1778:* P. 42, in George Rogers Clark Papers: 1771-1781, Ill. State Hist. Lib., Vol. VIII. Springfield, 1912.

    States: "If you have not retired to Draning's Lick I would give it as my opinion you had better make the place of Randavous at the *Big Bone Lick* where I am informed there will be a garrison erected as soon as Col. Bowman can get out—."

SMITH, Z. F.

169. *History of Kentucky:* Pp. 23, 24, 25, and 147. Louisville, 1892.

    A running account of Big Bone Lick, early visits by Douglas, McAfee, and others. Derived principally from L. and R. Collins, but with additions from McAfee.

TAYLOR, PHILIP FALL

170. *Earliest Surveys of Land in Kentucky:* P. 100 in Year Book of the Society of Colonial Wars in the Commonwealth of Kentucky. Louisville, 1917.

BIBLIOGRAPHY 151

Cites 1,000 acres surveyed for William Christian (Bundle 94, Ky. Land Office) on May 12, 1774, by John Floyd on a s. branch of the Ohio called Big Bone Creek, including the large Buffalo Lick and Salt Spring, being about 4 miles from the Ohio.

THOMPSON, ED. PORTER
171. *Young People's History of Kentucky:* P. 32. St. Louis, 1897.
Reference to Gist's trip to Big Bone Lick in 1751.

THWAITES, REUBEN GOLD
172. *Daniel Boone:* P. 87. New York, 1902.
Cites a French expedition as investigating Big Bone Lick in 1735. No such expedition is known and the reference may have been to De Longueil, but if so the date is in error.

173. *Early Western Travels, 1748-1846:* Vol. I, p. 135 (Croghan's Journal). Cleveland, 1904.
Colonel George Croghan's Journal of 1865 gives description of his visit to Big Bone Lick at that time.

THWAITES, REUBEN GOLD, AND KELLOGG, LOUISE PHELPS
174. *Documentary History of Dunmore's War 1774:* Thomas Hanson's Journal, 1774, p. 121. Madison, 1905.
Describes John Floyd's visit of May 12, 1774, to Big Bone Lick and survey of 1,000 acres about the lick for Col. William Christian.

TURNER, GEORGE
175. *Memoir on the Extraneous Fossils, Denominated Mammoth Bones, etc.:* No. LXXIV, pp. 510-518, Trans. of the Am. Phil. Soc. of Philadelphia, Vol. IV. Philadelphia, 1799.
Early description of Big Bone Lick and some of its fossil remains. Indian tradition as to the mammoth. (U. S. G. S. Lib.)

VARIOUS
176. Big Bone Lick: Draper MSS. Collection, Wisconsin State Historical Society. Madison, Wisconsin.
Many historical references to Big Bone Lick.

VILLEFOSSE, HERON DE
177. *Consederations sur les Fossiles, etc.:* 36 pp. Journal des Mines, No. 91. Paris (An. 12), 1804.
A Review of Blumenbach's *Handbuch der Naturgeschichte.* Refers to *"Mammut Ohioticum,* dit l'icognitum de l'Ohio, grand quadrupede" from Big Bone Lick. (U. S. G. S. Lib.)

WARREN, JOHN C.
178. *The Mastodon Giganteus of North America:* 260 pp., 31 Plates. Boston, 1855.

A very detailed and systematic description containing an important chronology on the scientific literature touching the mastodon. The Newburg mastodon. Numerous references to Big Bone Lick Mastodon fossils.

WEBB, WILLIAM S., AND FUNKHOUSER, W. D.
179. *Ancient Life in Kentucky:* Kentucky Geological Survey, Series VI, Vol. 34, pp. 40-46. Frankfort, 1928.
A good running account of the principal glacial and post glacial mammals recovered from Big Bone Lick.

WISTAR, CASPAR, JUN.
180. *Letter to Dr. William Goforth, from Philadelphia, December 1, 1806:* Appears in *The Navigator.* Pittsburgh, 1811.
Requests Goforth write the President of the United States (Thomas Jefferson) relative "to the bones of a large animal with claws," also as to the mammoth in his collection from Big Bone Lick.

181. *An Account of Two Heads Found in the Morass, Called Big Bone Lick, and Presented to the Society, by Mr. Jefferson:* No. XXXI, Trans. Amer. Philos. Soc. New. Ser., Vol. I, pp. 375-380. Plates X and XI, 1818.
Describes the skull of Bos bomifrons collected by General Clark for President Jefferson from Big Bone Lick. References to fossils sent to France by President Jefferson from the collection of General William Clark. Here is established the second species of extinct ox, to which Harlan later gave the name Bos bomifrons. Important paper. (U. S. G. S. Lib.)

WITHERS, SPENCER
182. *Oil and Gas Structural Geologic Map of Boone County, Kentucky:* Scale; 1:62,500, 10-foot contours, Kentucky Geological Survey, Series VI. Frankfort, 1931.
Shows detailed structural position of Big Bone Lick on the southern edge of the Big Bone Syncline.

WRIGHT, G. F.
183. *The Glacial Boundary in Western Pennsylvania, Ohio, Kentucky, Indiana, and Illinois:* U. S. Geol. Survey Bull. 58. Washington, 1890.

ZITTEL, KARL A. VON
184. *Grundzuge der Palaontologie (Palaozoologie):* II Ableilung: Vertebrata, p. 500. Munchen and Berlin, Germany, 1923.
Describes and figures (No. 618) Megalonyx Jeffersoni Leidy from the Pleistocene of (Big Bone Lick) Kentucky.

BIBLIOGRAPHY 153

NEWSPAPERS AND MAGAZINES

ANONYMOUS.

185. *Big Bone Lick Once Gathering Place of Chivalry of South:* Kentucky Weekly. Louisville, January 4, 1935.

Special story describing Big Bone Lick today and in the past. Famous fossil collections cited. John Thomas Lloyd, James Douglas, Dr. William Goforth, Thomas Ashe, Thomas Jefferson, M. Cuvier, etc., mentioned.

186. *Geology Talk Tonight:* Cincinnati Post, May 22, 1935.

Brief announcement of lecture by Dr. Willard Rouse Jillson, former State Geologist at Sinton Hotel, broadcast over Station WLW, Cincinnati, Ohio.

187. *Noted Geologist Will Be Heard:* Cincinnati Times-Star, May 10, 1935.

News story announcing lecture on "Big Bones of Northern Kentucky" to be given by Dr. Willard Rouse Jillson, at Sinton Hotel, Cincinnati, Ohio, May 22, 1935.

188. *Geologist Is to Speak About Kentucky Bones:* 1 Photo of Dr. Willard R. Jillson, Cincinnati Enquirer, May 14, 1935.

Announces lecture on big bones found in Northern Kentucky to be given at Sinton Hotel, Cincinnati, May 22, 1935.

189. *Geologist to Explain Fossils of Kentucky:* P. 9, 1 two-col. photo of Dr. Willard Rouse Jillson, Cincinnati Times-Star, May 15, 1935.

A news story outlining the work of a geologist and announcing Dr. Jillson's lecture in Cincinnati, May 22, 1935, on the fossils found at Big Bone Lick, Kentucky.

190. *Historical Big Bone Springs:* P. 1, Walton (Ky.) Advertiser, May 16, 1935.

Announces lecture on "Big Bones of Northern Kentucky" to be given in Sinton Hotel, Parlor F, May 22, 1935, by Willard Rouse Jillson, Sc. D.

191. *Booklet Published in 1801 Describes Big Bone (Ky.) Area:* P. 11, Cincinnati Enquirer, May 21, 1935.

A news story of general interest relative to Big Bone Lick and descriptions in *The Navigator.*

192. *Urge Preservation of Big Bone Lick:* Cincinnati Times-Star, May 23, 1935.

News account of a meeting at the Sinton Hotel, Cincinnati, Ohio, May 22, 1935. Notes on lecture by Dr. Willard Rouse Jillson.

BIBLIOGRAPHY

193. *Rescue Big Bone Lick for Posterity, etc.:* Cincinnati Enquirer, May 23, 1935.

  News account of a meeting at Sinton Hotel, Cincinnati, Ohio, May 22, 1935. Big Bone Lick Foundation is proposed.

194. *Big Bone Coming Into Its Own, etc.:* Walton Advertiser, Vol. 20, No. 32, p. 1, May 30, 1935.

  News story of movement to conserve Big Bone Lick. Personnel of Committee.

195. *Saving Big Bone Lick for Kentuckians:* Editorial, Lexington Herald, p. 4, Sunday, June 2, 1935.

  Editorial; favors new movement to conserve Big Bone Lick.

196. *Big Bone Area Soon to Be Acquired:* Cincinnati Enquirer, June 5, 1935.

  News story outlines plans for organization of Big Bone Lick Association and acquisition of 100 acres surrounding and including the celebrated lick.

COGHLAN, RALPH

197. *"Farthest North" for Kentucky:* Louisville Post, February 23, 1923.

  Describes Boone County and Big Bone Lick giving historical resume. James Douglas, Dr. William Goforth, Thomas Ashe, and others quoted from R. Collins.

DAUGHERTY, A. A.

198. *Mastodon Graveyard Boomed as Park Site:* 3 Illus., Louisville Times (Daily Magazine), September 20, 1935.

  Describes Big Bone Lick as it is today and outlines plans of Big Bone Lick Association; cites officers and principal workers.

DUNN, C. FRANK

199. *Memorializing Mary Ingles:* Lexington Herald, Sunday, June 16, 1935.

  Editorial recounting escape of Mary Ingles from Shawnee Indians at Big Bone Lick.

ENGLAND, J. RAY

200. *Kentucky Is Interesting Field for Student of Prehistoric Days:* P. 2, illustrated, The Kentucky Post, Sunday, February 14, 1932.

  A popular "Special" story on Big Bone Lick and its fossils based on a recent publication of the Kentucky Geological Survey by Edward M. Kindle.

HALLER, GRACE
201. *Directors Named by Association:* Cincinnati Enquirer, June 18, 1935.

   News story of the first meeting of the Big Bone Lick Association at Florence, Ky., June 17, 1935.

202. *Man and Mammoth at Big Bone Lick:* P. 4, Illustrated, Enquirer Sunday Magazine, Cincinnati, July 21, 1935.

RHODY, JAMES B.
203. *Movement on Foot to Preserve for Kentucky Fossils of Bones in State:* P. 1, Frankfort State Journal, June 6, 1935.

   News story outlining plans and personnel of conservationists at Big Bone Lick.

ROBERTSON, HARRISON (Editor)
204. *Kentucky Mastodons* (editorial): Courier-Journal, p. 6, November 27, 1924.

   Editorial. Comment on the recent discovery of a mastodon jaw and teeth near Sparta in Gallatin County and historical notes on Big Bone Lick with references to discovery in 1729; Mary Ingles and Christopher Gist.

ROUSE, ROBERT
205. *Plans for Establishing Museum at Big Bone Lick Formulated, etc.:* Lexington Herald, p. 1, Sunday, June 2, 1935.

   News story of a plan to build museum at Big Bone. Leaders in movement cited.

INDEX

INDEX

A

Adams, Samuel, 20.
Adler, Cyrus, 53.
African, 28.
Alces, 69, 116, 117.
Algonquins, 16.
Alleghenies, xv, 80, 84.
Allen, Wilson, 84.
America, 62.
American, 102.
Am. Jour. of Science, 61.
American Museum, 72.
Am. Phil. Society, 36, 37, 38, 40, 47, 49, 56.
American Revolution, 83.
Anthony, J. G., 105, 108.
Artiodactyla, 117.
Ashe, Thomas, 36, 37.
Atlantic, 80.
Auglaize River, 9.

B

Barton, Benjamin Smith, 9.
Batson, Mordicia, 90.
Beard, George F., 94.
Beaver Lick, 110, 116.
Beckner, Lucien, 7.
Bedford County, 79.
Bellin, Jacques Nicolas, 3, 4, 89.
Bibliography, 123, 125.
Big Bone, 17, 20, 21.
Big Bone, Map of, 103.
Bigelow, John, 28.
Bison, 68, 70, 72, 116, 117.

Blake, Dr., 37.
Bluegrass Region, 113.
Blue Licks, 87, 113.
Blue Ridge, 80.
Boone County, 90, 94, 110, 112, 113.
Boone, Daniel, 8, 16, 87.
Bootherium, 56, 63, 116, 117, 118.
Boquette, Colonel, 9.
Bourbon County, 84.
Breckinridges, 94.
British, 102.
British Museum, 65.
Brown, Dr. Barnum, 48, 72.
Buchanan, Mr., 105.
Buffalo, 3, 30.
Buffon, George L. de C., 32, 35.
Bullitt, Capt. Thomas, 20.
Bullitt's Lick, 87.
Bullock, William, 61, 65, 109.
Burne, R. H., 65.

C

Cambrian, 112.
Canada, 73.
Carneal, Davis, 90.
Carneal, Thomas, 90.
Carnivora, 118.
Celeron, M. de, 4.
Cenozoic, 111.
Cervalces, 69, 117.
Cervus, 69, 71, 116, 117.
Chappe, Abbe, 29.
Chard, 88.
Chili, 33.

INDEX

Christian, Anna, 81.
Christian, William, 21, 76, 77, 78, 80, 81, 82.
Cincinnati, xvi, 36, 38, 40, 60, 88, 91, 105, 106, 109, 110, 111, 112.
Cincinnati, Western Mus. Soc., 60.
Civil War, 62.
Clark, Capt. William, 47, 48, 51, 54, 56, 59.
Clark, Gen. G. R., 49, 50, 102.
Clark, General William, 71.
Clarksville, 49, 54.
Clay, Henry, 95.
Clay House, 95.
Clays, 94.
Clifford, John D., 60.
Cline, Dr., 35.
Colland, General, 36.
Collectors, 57, 59.
Collins, Lewis, 36, 59, 93, 95.
Collins, Richard, 8, 20, 63, 87.
Collinson, Peter, 9, 31.
Colquohoun, Mr., 92, 93.
Cooper, William, 36, 60, 62, 102, 103, 105, 108, 115, 116.
Courtanvaux, Marquis de, 30.
Covington, 95, 111.
Cozzens, I., 60.
Cramer, Zadok, 37, 38, 39, 91.
Crawford, Hugh, 5, 6.
Cresswell, Nicholas, 21, 22.
Crittendens, 94.
Croghan, Col. George, 8, 15, 16, 27, 28, 30, 119.
Cumberland Gap, 16.
Cuttaway River, 7.
Cuvier, Georges, 36, 108.

D

Dandridge, William, 80, 81.
Daniel, Robert, 82, 83.
Debrett, J., 34.
Deeds, 75, 77.
Deer, 3, 23, 30.
Detroit, 16.
Dicotyles, 69.
Discovery, 3.
Douglas, James, 21, 77, 89, 90.
Dublin, 37.

E

Earickson, Benjamin, 83.
Eden Group, 111.
Edentata, 117.
Egerton Collection, 66.
Elephant, 15, 19, 20, 22, 23, 28, 29, 35.
Elephas, 63, 65, 69, 72, 116, 117.
Elk, 3, 71.
England, 36, 62.
Enniskillen Collection, 66, 67.
Equus, 63, 69, 71, 107, 116, 117.
Eskippakithiki, 7.
Europe, 35, 40, 42.
Exploration, 3.

F

Falconer, C., 66, 67.
Falls of Ohio, 6, 102.
Fayette County, 81.
Filson Club, 70.
Filson, John, 4, 27, 32.
Fincastle County, 77.
Findley, John (See Finley), 7.
Finley, John, 16.

INDEX

Finnell, Capt. Benjamin, 61, 65.
Florence, 95.
Flower, W. H., 65.
Floyd, John, 21, 76, 77, 78, 79.
Fort du Quesne, 9, 30.
Fort Massac, 55.
Fort Niagara, 3.
Fort Pitt, 15, 16, 20.
Fossil Collecting, 25, 27.
France, 49, 51, 62.
France, Nat. Inst. of, 51, 56.
Frankfort, 76, 77, 78.
Franklin, Benjamin, 9, 28, 29, 31, 32.
French, 102.
French and Indian War, 9.

G

Gage, General, 16.
Geology, 32, 99, 101, 125.
Germany, 62.
Gist, Christopher, 5, 27.
Glacial Age, xv.
Goforth, Dr. William, 36, 37, 38, 39, 43, 47, 91.
Gordon, Capt. Harry, 9, 16, 19, 28.
Grants, 75, 77.
Graves, Mr., 61.
Gum Lick, 107.
Gunpowder Creek, 116.

H

Hamilton Landing, 95.
Hanson, Thomas, 21, 77, 79.
Harrison, General W. H., 36, 119.

Harvard, 62, 64, 68, 115.
Harvie, John, 80, 81.
Havana, 55.
Hay, O. P., 117.
Herbivora, 110.
History, 125.
Hite, Isaac, 90.
Horse, 70.
Hunter, Dr., 20, 34, 35.
Hutchins, Thomas, 16, 17, 19.
Hyhan, Mr., 65.

I

Igneous Rocks, 112.
Illinoian Stage, 114, 115.
Illinois River, 10.
Imlay, Capt. Gilbert, 34.
Indian, 21, 28, 88, 90, 101.
Indian Old Fields, 8.
Indiana, 94, 111, 121.
Inglis, Mary, 8, 87.

J

Jefferson County, 82, 89.
Jefferson, Thomas, 10, 35, 36, 38, 40, 47, 48, 50, 52, 54, 55, 56, 59, 78, 84, 91.
Jillson, Willard Rouse, vi, ix, x, xvi, 4, 78, 80, 84, 89, 91, 113.

K

Kansan Epoch, 114.
Karleskind, Lorene C., 72.
Kenton, Simon, 87.
Kentucky, 121.

INDEX

Kentucky Geological Survey, 69, 113.
Kentucky, Univ. of, 69.
Kickapoos, 16.
Kindle, E., 16, 36.
Kinkead, Ludie J., 83.

L

Land Surveys, 75, 77.
LaSalle, Robert, 11.
Lee, Capt. Hancock, 22.
Leidy, Joseph, 62, 115.
Lery, Chaussegros de, 3.
Lewis, Capt., 47, 48, 55.
Lexington, 60, 95.
Licking River, 113.
Lincoln's Inn Fields, 65.
Liverpool, 36.
Lloyd, John Thomas, xi.
Lloyd, John Uri, xvi.
London, 19, 28, 32, 34, 35, 65.
Longueil, Capt. Charles Lemoyne de, 3, 4.
Louis XIII, 102.
Louisiana, 4, 102.
Lyceum of Nat. History, 62.
Lydekker, Richard, 66.
Lyell, Sir Charles, 62, 105.

M

Magazines, 153.
Maimon, 33.
Mammoth, 47, 49, 51, 60, 65, 70.
Mammouth, 35.
Mammut, 117.
Mantell Collection, 66.

Marshalls, 94.
Maryland, 19.
Mascoutins, 16.
Massachusetts, 68.
Mastodon, 55, 61, 63, 65, 69, 70, 72, 73, 115.
Maysville, 111.
McAfee, George, 20.
McAfee, James, 20.
McAfee, Robert, 20.
McCoun, James, 20.
McDowells, 94.
Medicinal Springs, 4.
Megalonyx, 69, 73, 116, 117, 118.
Merrill, George P., 52.
Messozoic, 111.
Metamorphic Rocks, 112.
Miami, Big, 4, 15, 27.
Miami River, 9, 27.
Miamis, 27.
Miller, A. M., 32.
Mississippi River, 40, 90, 91.
Mitchell, C. G., 17.
Molini, M., 29.
Monroe, Prof., 36.
Montgomery County, 79, 80.
Monticello, 51, 53.
Montreal, 3.
Moore, J. B., 70, 71.
Moore, J. Percey, 71.
Mosby, J., 80, 81.
Moses, 59.
Myers, Jacob, 84.
Mylodon, 69, 117.

N

Navigator, 37, 38, 91.
Nebraskan Epoch, 114.

INDEX 163

Newberne, 107.
New France, 3, 102.
New Holland, 34.
New Orleans, 36, 38, 49, 50, 51, 54, 90.
Newport, 62, 111.
Newspapers, 153.
New York, 28, 30, 61, 91, 102, 108.
New York State, 72.
Nicholas County, 113.
North America, 106.
North Carolina, 19, 107.

O

Odocoileus, 69, 116, 117.
Ohio, 30, 94, 111, 121.
Ohio Land Company, 5, 6.
Ohio Valley, 3, 4, 87, 102, 113, 114.
Old Britain, 27.
Ordovician, 111, 112, 114.
Ovibos, 69, 72.
Owen, David Dale, 62.
Owen, Sir Richard, 67.

P

Paleontology, 53, 91, 99, 101, 125.
Paleozoic, 112.
Paris, 4.
Passiers, Joseph, 22.
Peale, Rembrandt, 37.
Peccary, 116.
Pennsylvania, 15, 19, 32.
Perissodactyla, 117.
Peru, 28.

Philadelphia, 4, 38, 40, 43, 47, 50, 51, 53, 91.
Philadelphia, Acad. of Nat. Science, 56, 60.
Phinnel, Mr. (See Finnell), 106.
Pickawillany, 9, 27.
Pittsburgh, 15, 37, 39.
Platygonus, 116.
Pleistocene, 32, 63, 64, 111, 112, 114, 117, 118, 120.
Preston, Col. Wm., 77.
Proboscidia, 118, 119.

R

Rafinesque, 60, 62, 94.
Rangifer, 69, 117.
Ravenel, W. de C., 73.
Recent, 111, 114.
Richardson, Dr., 38.
Rochester, 73.
Rochester, Univ. of, 72.
Romer, 68.
Roots, Edmund W., 84.
Ross, David, 47, 48, 77, 79, 80, 81, 84, 90, 91.
Royal Coll. of Surgeons, 36, 65.
Royal Society, 28, 31.
Rule, Lucien, 89.

S

Saint Peter, 112, 114.
Salt, 88.
Salt Making, 85, 87.
Salt River, 87.
Salt Springs, 4, 20.
Sandusky, "Eph," 89.
Sandusky, Jacob, 90.

INDEX

Shaler, Nathaniel S., 62, 63, 64, 109, 115, 116.
Shane, Rev. J. D., 89.
Shelbourne, Lord, 9, 16, 28, 30, 31.
Shideler, W. H., 113.
Siberia, 29, 30.
Silliman, Benjamin, 61.
Skeletons, 30, 110.
Smith, Albert H., 29, 32.
Smith, John, 90.
Smith, J. A., 62.
Smith, Robert, 4, 5, 6.
Smith, Stephen, 83.
Social Activities, 85, 87.
St. Clair, Gen. Arthur, 88.
St. Mary's, 55.
Symbos, 116, 117.

T

Tapir, 71.
Tapirus, 71, 117.
Tartary, 33.
Taylor, Hancock, 20.
Thruston, R. C. B., 70.
Todds, 94.
Toulmin-Smith Collection, 68.
Travel Journals, 13, 15.
Twigtwee Town, 4.

U

Union, 95, 110.
United States, 73.
Ursus, 69, 118.

V

Virginia, 19, 91.

W

Wabash River, 10, 16, 27.
Walton, 95.
Wards Nat. Sc. Establishment, 73.
Warren Museum, 115.
Washington, 47, 49, 50, 51, 52, 53.
Waters, Richard Jones, 82, 83.
West Virginia, 93.
Wetherill, John Price, 60.
White Cave, 60.
White House, 71.
Williams, 80, 81.
Williamson, Horace G., xi.
Wilmington, 32.
Wistar, Dr. Caspar, 38, 39, 40, 47, 51, 52, 53, 55, 65, 91.
Withers, Spencer, 112.
Woolper Creek, 116.

Y

Yale College, 61.
Yarmouth, 114.
Young, Prof. D. M., 69.

www.ingramcontent.com/pod-product-compliance
Lightning Source LLC
Chambersburg PA
CBHW060525080526
44586CB00012B/617